D0398328

A **Survival Guide** to
Managing
Employees from Hell

A Survival Guide to
Managing
Employees from Hell

Handling Idiots, Whiners, Slackers, and Other Workplace Demons

Gini Graham Scott, Ph.D.

RETIRÉ DE LA COLLECTION UNIVERSELLE
Bibliothèque et Archives nationales du Québec

AMACOM
American Management Association
New York • Atlanta • Brussels • Chicago • Mexico City • San Francisco
Shanghai • Tokyo • Toronto • Washington, D.C.

Special discounts on bulk quantities of AMACOM books are
available to corporations, professional associations, and other
organizations. For details, contact Special Sales Department,
AMACOM, a division of American Management Association,
1601 Broadway, New York, NY 10019.
Tel: 212-903-8316. Fax: 212-903-8083.
E-mail: specialsls@amanet.org
Website: www. amacombooks.org/go/specialsales
To view all AMACOM titles go to: www.amacombooks.org

This publication is designed to provide accurate and authoritative
information in regard to the subject matter covered. It is sold with the
understanding that the publisher is not engaged in rendering legal,
accounting, or other professional service. If legal advice or other expert
assistance is required, the services of a competent professional person
should be sought.

Library of Congress Cataloging-in-Publication Data

Scott, Gini Graham.
    A survival guide to managing employees from hell : handling idiots, whiners,
slackers, and other workplace demons / Gini Graham Scott.
        p.   cm.
    Includes index.
    ISBN-10: 0-8144-7408-X
    ISBN-13: 978-0-8144-7408-2
    1. Problem employees—Case studies.   2. Supervision of employees.   I. Title.

HF5549.5.E42S36   2007
658.3'045—dc22

                                                    2006019310

© 2007 Gini Graham Scott, Ph.D.
All rights reserved.
Printed in the United States of America.

This publication may not be reproduced,
stored in a retrieval system,
or transmitted in whole or in part,
in any form or by any means, electronic,
mechanical, photocopying, recording, or otherwise,
without the prior written permission of AMACOM,
a division of American Management Association,
1601 Broadway, New York, NY 10019.

Printing number

10   9   8   7   6   5   4   3   2   1

Contents

Introduction   vii

Part I: Bad Attitude   1

  1. One Tough Babe   3
  2. A Serious Threat   8
  3. Prima Donna   14
  4. The Arrogant A**Hole   19
  5. Cultural Chasm   23
  6. Negative Nelly or Ned   28
  7. Spilling the Beans   34

Part II: Incompetent   41

  8. The Impossible Intern   43
  9. Damaged Goods   48
10. Getting It Wrong   53
11. Friends Forever   58
12. Protected by the Big Boss   63
13. Last to Know   67

Part III: Personal Issues   73

14. The Sensitive Soul   75
15. One Problem After Another   80

16. Too Much, Too Soon   85
17. Got Drugs?   91
18. In the Drink   95
19. Sick and Tired   99
20. Scary Employee   103
21. A Handful of Sex Problems   107

Part IV: Trust and Honesty   111

22. Liar, Liar!   113
23. It's the Little Things   118
24. Over a Barrel   124
25. Con Job   130
26. Pay or Play   135
27. A Favor Backfires   140
28. On the Side   145

Part V: Communication   151

29. Communication Breakdown   153
30. What Are You Talking About?   158
31. Silence Is Golden   163
32. Who's in Charge Here?   167
33. When the Cat's Away   172
34. Putting the Customer First   177

Part VI: Putting It All Together   181

35. Bad Employee or Bad Boss?   183
36. How Bad Is Your Employee (or Employees)?
    A Self-Assessment Quiz   188
37. Knowing How to Deal   193

Appendix: Dealing with Difficult Employees Grid   213

Index   219
About the Author   229

Introduction

Just as virtually everyone has had some bad bosses over the course of their career, so company owners, managers, and other employees have commonly had an experience with a difficult employee. Bad employees can cause major headaches for their bosses, especially if they are not dealt with in a timely and decisive way. They can also negatively affect the entire workplace, contributing to lowered morale, reduced productivity and higher turnover.

Some bosses feel stymied about what kind of action they can take, particularly in this age of empowered employees, where lawsuits for wrongful termination, harassment, and creating an oppressive workplace environment are all too common. How can you deal with a difficult employee in such an atmosphere? Are you able to fire that employee if other measures to correct the problem don't succeed?

Whatever the problem, there are many things you can do to maintain control—from carefully interviewing and checking out the employee before you hire, to meeting with the employee at the first sign of trouble, to keeping a detailed paper trail when an employee looks like trouble.

What makes a difficult employee? They come in all varieties and combinations. Many bad employees would create problems in any situation or workplace. But sometimes what makes for a difficult employee in one working culture—such as a loner in a highly social, team-player environment—may make for a highly productive and valuable employee in another setting. For example, that same loner in a high-tech company, where creative employees are free to create at their own pace, may thrive and become a highly valuable contributor. So difficulties with employees can be shaped by the working environment, as well as by the particular personality traits of the employee and others with whom he or she works.

Just as bad bosses are determined by subjective measures—what employees think about them—so, too, are difficult employees, in this case by what their boss and other employees think about them. In turn, there are different strategies for dealing with these different types of difficult employees. The optimum approach depends not only on the type of difficulty, but also on the interplay of personalities, politics, systems, and structure in the workplace.

In this book, you'll encounter all sorts of difficult employees, some with multiple reasons for being difficult. For example, here are some of those you'll meet: the bully, the know-it-all, the busybody and gossip, the backstabber, the incompetent, the sensitive soul, the emotional wreck, the slow poke, and the poor communicator. You may find some of these many different types in your own office.

You'll also learn a series of tools for making the best of a difficult situation. Depending on the situation, you might do more training or assign a mentor, provide a warning, assign more or fewer tasks, observe and monitor, transfer or demote, dock the employee's pay, or ultimately fire the bad employee.

A Survival Guide for Managing Employees from Hell is designed to help you identify the different types of bad employees and decide what to do about them. As in the previous books in this series—*A Survival Guide for Working with Bad Bosses* and *A Survival Guide for Working with Humans*—it draws on real-life stories. I've learned of these tales—and many others—in the course of consulting, conducting workshops and seminars, writing columns and books, being an exhibitor at conventions, and just talking to people about their experiences in the workplace.

Each chapter uses a mix of problem-solving and conflict-resolution techniques, along with methods such as visualization, analytical reasoning, and intuitive assessment—and a strong dose of using your own common sense.

In general, you'll find that being open and honest and straightforward where you can be is often the best policy. Doing so creates a good foundation for trust and predictability that helps employees know what's required, expected, and where they stand. Your goal should always be to find a balanced solution that will allow for the greatest success. That means you need to figure out what is causing an employee to be difficult and what actions are most likely to lead to improvements if possible, while keeping in mind that not every difficult employee will respond to even the best of strategies. In those cases, the optimum solution is to diplomatically let the employee go. You will help the employee save face and reduce the potential for workplace disruptions, as well as for potential legal or other repercussions from a disgruntled ex-employee.

Whatever the situation, it's important to recognize that no one approach or solution fits all, just as in dealing with any type of workplace problem. You have to adapt your options not only to the situation, but to your own style and personality, as well as that of the employee. You also have to consider if this is an isolated case of one difficult employee—one bad apple in the barrel—or whether the problem involves others, such as when two or more employees are creating a problem because of what happens when they work together. This can make a difference in whether to seek a group or an individual solution, or even make some systematic or structural changes in the workplace. Also, different principles, strategies, and tactics will work best for you at different times, based on what's happening at the company and whether you are the top boss or you have other executives above you.

Consider these chapters to be like a catalog of different tools for dealing with different types of difficult employees. In keeping with this catalog approach, each chapter features the following tools:

- ➲ An introductory paragraph highlighting the difficulty.
- ➲ A short story about one or more owners or managers who faced this type of employee. The stories are real, but the identities, companies, and employee names have been changed to protect the guilty—and the innocent.
- ➲ A quiz with a list of possible responses so you can think about what you might do in a given situation. You can even use this as a management training exercise or game to discuss this issue with others and compare your responses.

➲ A discussion of how these owners or managers chose to respond to their difficult employee or how they might respond.

➲ A series of three or more take-aways to highlight the chapter's key points.

As you read about how other people have dealt with difficult employees, you might think about how you can apply these strategies yourself or use them to advise a friend or associate with a difficult employee.

I hope you enjoy this survival guide, and I hope it helps you improve your situation at work. Read on and meet the many different kinds of difficult employees, some of whom might seem like ornery animals disrupting your carefully coordinated office zoo. Feel free to explore and visit these different employees in any order, and as you do, think about what you can learn about how to deal with your own difficult employee or employees. Think of yourself as the zookeeper. The better you learn to deal with the animals that become hard to handle, the happier and more productive everyone at the zoo will be.

If you have your own questions, feel free to visit the section of the website devoted to this book at www.workingwithhumans.com/difficultemployees and send them to me.

Part I

Bad Attitude

1 One Tough Babe

An especially difficult employee is the one who is extremely obnoxious with everyone—always acting tough and coming on like gangbusters. Such behavior can be even more of a problem when he or she isn't directly your employee, but does work for you. You need the employee to do a good job to support your own work and your staff's work, but you aren't directly in charge of the person. So with a mixture of bluster and manipulative charm, the employee can literally end up controlling you.

That's the situation which Alice faced when she became a manager for a loan brokerage company. Her job was to manage the work of a half dozen loan brokers who spent much of the time out in the field, as well as coordinate everyday office operations. One of the employees who worked in the office, but not directly under Alice's supervision, was Cherise. She processed the loans, which mainly involved filling out the detailed documentation required for each loan package so it would be approved by the bank. This was a highly technical job and Cherise had the skills to do a good job, which she parlayed into a free pass to run roughshod over everyone in the office. The one exception was the company owner, to whom she reported directly. With him, she turned on the charm and the tears to excuse the upset and chaos she created by dumping on everyone else.

Alice had her first brush with what working with Cherise would be like when Cherise came into her office, leaned over, and said, "Listen, babe, I'm not afraid of you." Then, in a sudden change of tone, she continued sweetly, "That said, I'll do everything I can to help you be successful." Alice was quickly filled in by the other employees who described their repeated run-ins with Cherise. As Alice related, "Cherise had a kind of destroy and conquer approach. She saw everyone as the enemy and she looked for everyone's weaknesses and tried to exploit those."

Cherise also dressed the part, a mix of tough and sexy. She wore leather pants and skirts, tight blouses, stiletto heels, and had long flowing hair. She rode a Harley motorcycle to work and revved it up when she arrived at the office; she also owned two pit bulls. "She was one tough cookie," Alice commented, "and she wanted everyone to know it. Though she was part of the office I was managing, she wanted to make it very clear from the outset that she was not working for me."

It was a schizophrenic kind of working arrangement that made for craziness. Typically, Cherise would come in late, about 10:30 a.m., and leave early, about 3:30 p.m. During that time she was like a hurricane sweeping through the office, laying waste to all in her path. "She would scream at me and the loan brokers that things weren't ready. She would yell at the vendors—the bankers who were taking the completed loan applications to the potential investors—that they hadn't completed their part of the applications right.

If anyone complained to the head honcho about her behavior and he spoke to her about this, she would go into her "poor me" act, even though she was earning about $200,000 a year. Acting as the abused party rather than the abuser, she would sob about how much pressure she was under at work, as well as at home where she had problems with her house, her sometimes violent boyfriend, and her ailing mother for whom she was caring. Each meeting led her to describe a new bunch of problems to the boss. Her litany of tribulations worked, since she had been doing such specialized one-of-a-kind work for him for over 15 years. After one of their talks, her tirades at the office would calm down for a short time, but then a week or two later, they would start up again.

From time to time, Alice tried to confront Cherise about her latest tirade, such as telling her to stop yelling at the front desk people—who did report to Alice—but Cherise wouldn't listen. "Instead she was real snippy," Alice said. "She would say, 'Okay, I will. Now get out.' And then she would do what she had always done. I was supposed to manage her, along with the rest of the office, but I didn't have the authority to fire her. So I felt really stuck in knowing what to do."

What Should Alice Do?

In Alice's place, what would you do and why? What do you think the outcomes of these different options would be? Here are some possibilities:

➲ Since just talking to Cherise yourself hasn't worked, get together all of the loan brokers in the office and go talk to her as a group, asking her to change.

➲ Tape record Cherise's tirades, so you have proof of what she has been doing to take to the company owner.

➲ Have a meeting with the loan brokers in which you tell them to not take Cherise's screaming fits personally because she is doing this with everyone.

➲ Bring several loan brokers with you to a meeting with the owner so they can help you present a case about Cherise's rants and mistreatment of the other employees.

➲ Learn how to process loans yourself so the loan brokers don't have to use Cherise to process their loans.

➲ Find an outside loan processor to handle the loan processing. Tell the company owner that you and the loan brokers would prefer an alternative and you think this will result in more effective operations and a better bottom line.

➲ Talk to the bankers Cherise has been dealing with to get documentation from them about how Cherise has been abusive to them.

➲ Other?

In this case, since reasoning with Cherise yourself hasn't worked, one strategy might be the strength-in-numbers approach in going to Cherise with other loan brokers to get her to control her abusive behavior. Then tell her you will go to the company owner if she doesn't stop, and do so if conditions don't improve. At the same time, having a meeting with the loan brokers to show them your support might help with office morale while you are all trying to deal with this problem.

If you do go to the owner, take a more proactive approach to show the owner how serious the problem is and how he might resolve it. This might be particularly important in this case, since the owner has let the situation go on for years. Cherise has been getting away with this behavior for so long she feels she can trample on others in the office with impunity. So you have to make a convincing case in order to get the owner to change anything. Besides going to the owner as a group to describe the problem, you might tape some of Cherise's tirades to show how truly abusive her behavior has been.

It may not be practical for you to learn these specialized skills yourself, and doing such work might detract from your own responsibilities in managing the office. However, you might look for outside loan processors who could be replacements for Cherise so the owner doesn't feel he has to continue to depend on her to do the work.

So what did Alice actually do to resolve the problem? In her case, nature fortunately intervened, which completely changed the office dynamics. Ironically, one of Cherise's pit bulls pulled her middle finger out of joint, so she arrived at work with her finger in a straight-up locked position. As a result, she couldn't do her job, which required extensive writing and typing. After she left for several months to have corrective surgery, the company owner terminated her and found someone else to replace her. Even more ironically, despite her high salary and short hours, she sued the owner for ten years of overtime pay, claiming he overworked her because she wasn't paid for her lunch hours. Eventually, the case got settled. Of course, Alice and the loan brokers were just glad she was gone. Even so, as Alice pointed out, "The lawsuit at the end showed she wouldn't let go. Even when she was no longer in the company, she was still trying to control and intimidate."

Today's Take-Aways

☑ Sometimes the law of karma may really come to your aid and take care of a very difficult problem for you, though you can only hope and pray!

☑ If someone tries to be tough and intimidating, you may find that strength in numbers helps you to be tough and intimidating back.

☑ If there is a long-standing problem, you may need to stir up the standing waters to bring about change.

☑ If you have a go to a top boss or company owner about a long-term serious problem, you can be more persuasive if you don't just tell. Instead, bring others along and use demonstrations to show and tell.

2 A Serious Threat

What do you do if you feel an employee you want to discipline or fire is a serious threat? This is a situation that could happen when an employee is mentally unstable, physically powerful, part of a culture of violence, or even has criminal connections. Sometimes employers can get into this situation if they miss the danger signs when they are first hiring an employee. Other times it can happen if they hire someone through a government outreach program that is encouraging the hiring of troubled youths, former drug addicts, or ex-cons. Such programs provide a great opportunity for individuals who otherwise might not be employed to turn their lives around. They work well much of the time, but once in awhile, someone slips through who is not ready for primetime employment.

That's what happened to Joy and her husband, Dave, who had been working as independent contractors in construction administration for 14 years. The job involved overseeing contracts for large public works clients, such as the city water company. After they became too busy to handle a job themselves, one water company asked them to hire a construction clerk and told them exactly who they wanted to hire: James, a strapping, 6'9", street-savvy former high school football star, who was a drinking buddy of the manager of the project. Another reason the water company wanted to hire James was because he would help meet the requirements for hiring rehabilitated members of the local community, since he was an ex-convict who lived in the city. James had served prison time for a violent assault during a drunken brawl outside a bar. And supposedly he had worked as a clerk on a similar job in the past.

Since Joy knew she had to hire James to get the contract, she conducted only a brief interview with him and didn't do any background check with his past employers. She also overlooked any warning signs, such as when James asked about and seemed more interested in the vacation time and medical benefits than in the actual work he would be doing.

The problems started soon after James started on the project. His job involved handling all the documents generated by the project. While there wasn't much to do in the first few weeks, he didn't prepare for the coming deluge by setting up any kind of filing or organizational system. In fact, Joy wasn't sure what James did, since James didn't keep her informed; he just reassured Joy when she called each week that things were going well. And since Vicky, the project manager, didn't report any complaints—at least not then— Joy thought things were fine. However, James quickly abused his vacation and sick leave days, by using up five out of ten days in the first month of the project, and the rest in the second month.

At the same time, Vicky became afraid of controlling or disciplining James. When she set up some job requirements or corrected him, James would seem reluctant to make the requested changes, and frequently joked, "Hey, if you don't watch out, I'll throw you in the creek," referring to the large creek which roared by about 100 feet from the water building. Though James said the words in jest, there was a scary subtext, as if he might really do it.

Then, more problems developed in the second month when one of James's two sons, 15-year-old Jeremy, got shot five times during a drug deal gone bad, and his cousin was beaten up and later died. So James needed some extra time off to deal with that, and Joy went in to sub for him for the first time. When she did, she discovered that James hadn't set up any filing system, and when she checked the computer, she found a badly written resume that James had prepared for his other son. "I was really shocked," Joy said. "The English was so bad, and I was surprised because James had held a similar job before on another city project without any complaints about him. But then when I called his former employer, I learned that she was a quiet, very passive boss. James had done minimal work there, and pretty much chose his own hours and what to do. It was as if his boss was afraid to say or do anything to set limits or rules.''

Yet, for a time, Joy and Vicky tried to support James because of the shooting of his son. But then, when Joy had to go in to sub for James again to file and organize some documents, Vicky and an inspector working on the project explained to her that James just wasn't working out. The next day, when James came to work, Joy went in to train him and found the experience unnerving. "He was very defensive," Joy explained. "He was wearing a dark sweatshirt and dark glasses, and he argued with me about his performance. He didn't want to listen and he was resentful. He denied doing anything wrong or taking advantage of anyone." So Joy, feeling a little threatened at trying to do more, simply spent a few hours showing James the filing system she had set up for him, then left.

Finally, things came to a head two weeks later, when Vicky and the inspector asked Joy to come in again and told her all the things that James wasn't doing. Then they told her, "You'll have to fire him." Moreover, they didn't want Joy to replace James with anyone else because "we have no budget for that anymore." Just to be sure that this situation with James wouldn't hurt their stellar reputation with the water district, Joy contacted the city's regulatory agency in charge of the outreach program and sent a letter of explanation.

Then she had to deal with firing James. Since Vicky and the inspector didn't want James to return, Joy packed up his belongings. But she didn't want to bring them to James's house or have James come to her house because, as she explained, "I felt threatened by him. I felt that James was hiding behind humor in his threats to Vicky, such as saying, 'I could throw you in the creek,' and I knew his son had a gun and was part of the drug world. So in case the firing upset him, I wanted to meet him in a neutral place."

Joy called James and told him that "the district informed me that I have to fire you." At once, James began pleading about how he would have no job and medical coverage, which he desperately needed because of his high blood pressure. Joy explained she didn't have any choice, but offered to let him file for unemployment even though she didn't have to because she was firing James for cause. Then she arranged to meet him at the water district's conference room to return his belongings, and she brought her husband to the meeting, afraid to meet James alone.

She found that James's anger was directed at Vicky and the inspector, not at her, and she just listened as James griped on and on about them; then she gave him his belongings. And afterward, she felt relieved that James wasn't angry at her. "It was scary because of his size and the criminal element in his family. I felt he could really harm me or my husband if he wanted to. In looking back, I feel like he was someone who worked the system. He had no work ethic and he didn't have the word processing or other skills to do the job. But he was able to manipulate and frighten people to get his way."

What Might Joy Have Done Differently?

Was there anything that Joy might have done differently, knowing that she had to hire James if she wanted to get the contract job? In Joy's place, what would you do and why? What do you think the outcomes of these different options would be? Here are some possibilities:

- ⮑ Don't take the job if the only way you can get it is to hire James.

- ⮑ Provide some extra training and supervision for James—even if you aren't expected to—to make sure he is doing the job the way it should be done properly.

- ⮑ Give James guidelines in the beginning about how much of his ten-day vacation or sick time he can use during the year, such as one day the first month, two days the second month, three days the third month, etc., so he can't abuse the privilege.

- ⮑ Ask Vicky, the project manager, to give you a weekly report for the first few weeks so you can check if things are working out and if James is doing what you expect him to be doing.

- ⮑ Stop in once or twice unexpectedly during the first few weeks to check on what James is doing and learn if he needs any help with the work.

- ⮑ Take James's joking threats seriously and discuss your concerns immediately with Vicky, as soon as she mentions them.

➲ Ask Vicky to keep records of what James is doing.

➲ As soon as you find through early checking that James isn't
doing the work and won't respond to your efforts to correct and
train him, tell Vicky that you think James should be terminated
and replaced with someone else. Don't wait for Vicky to come to
you asking to fire James.

➲ Other?

This is certainly a tricky situation because of social and public policies supporting the hiring of disadvantaged employees. Some people
may use these policies to manipulate the system and keep employers
afraid of requiring them to do a full day's work or terminating them
for poor performance. Ideally, it would be best to not hire an employee as soon as you sense that employee means trouble, which is
what Joy sensed about James. But in some industries, this may not
be possible because of industry practices, contracts, or other factors.
You may need the work and so you hope for the best, which was the
situation Joy and her husband were in.

However, once an employee becomes a serious threat, it is important to take proper action to carefully terminate that employee to
get him or her out of the office, and then act to reduce the chances
of any retaliation. In addition, if you have any evidence that the
threat may be carried out, call the authorities so you get your fears
on record. If necessary, ask for a restraining order, too, or warn others who might be at risk. For example, when James spoke about his
anger at Vicky and the inspector, Joy might have passed on a warning about James's anger since it could possibly lead to his trying to
hurt them or the project in some way.

Joy might have also instituted a hands-on training program for
the first day or days that James was on the job, even if the project
manager was in charge. Then, as she found gaps in James's knowledge needed for the work, she could do more intensive training in
that area. Even though James supposedly had worked on a similar
job without complaints from his superiors, Joy shouldn't have taken
anything for granted; instead, she should have observed firsthand
what James did and compared that to what James was supposed to
do. It might be particularly helpful to use modeling in training
James, such as by showing James how he should set up a filing sys-

tem by creating the first few files, and afterward observing how he does on his own.

Possibly, too, when Joy found James being resistant and resentful, she might have called him on his behavior. She could have asked him to take off his dark glasses because that was making it hard to talk to him, emphasizing that it was important to listen in order to learn how to do the job well. Maybe, too, she might have called out James when she sensed he was being resentful by saying she sensed James felt this way and hoped to find a way to make the job more satisfying for him. She might have also pointed out how James was risking his job if things didn't change. And she might have pointed out her own efforts to help James when his son was shot, but that now that he was back at work, he needed to put the incident behind him and focus on doing good work.

Even if such strategies might not have worked in the end, it was worthwhile to try to be more proactive in looking for problems and making changes along the way, rather than waiting for things to unravel.

Today's Take-Aways

- ☑ If you think an employee may be a threat to you, try to avoid hiring that employee and risking that this threat may become real.

- ☑ Check on what an employee is doing on the first day or days of the job, even if the employee claims to have done the same kind of work before. You'll feel more reassured if you confirm it for yourself and if the employee is wrong, you can take preventative acts to train or supervise the employee more closely right away.

- ☑ If you fear a hostile confrontation with an employee you have to seriously discipline or terminate, find a neutral, well-observed place to have your meeting—such as a centrally located conference room or busy restaurant—and arrange for someone else to join you at the meeting. Don't get into a situation where you are alone.

- ☑ Document, document, document what happens each day, just in case you have to justify your reasons for firing the employee if he or she decides to challenge you in court or through some kind of administrative hearing.

3 Prima Donna

Sometimes a promotion can unleash the inner prima donna, such as when a previously well-performing employee is suddenly thrust into a supervisory or management position. It's as if the rush of power becomes intoxicating, and the person loves being in charge. He or she relishes the opportunity to now be the one pulling the strings and gaining admiration and love from others for what he or she can do. The situation is a little like that of the opera prima donna, who has become the center of attention and loves the starring and commanding role.

That's the situation Vince, who ran a small hospital, faced when he promoted Vivian, one of his nurses, to be a shift supervisor. Before her promotion, Vivian had been an excellent nurse, beloved by her patients for her extra care and attention. But when Vince promoted Vivian to supervisor based on her exemplary record as a nurse, problems soon ensued. Vivian transferred her desire to care for others and receive love and admiration from her patients to the staff members she supervised. Unfortunately, though the staff loved her, she went the extra mile at the expense of office productivity and budget considerations, and Vince was soon fuming.

For example, she made herself friends with all the staff members while neglecting the records she was supposed to keep. As Vince explained: "Everyone loved her. Every week she was doing different things to make the staff members happy, like giving them extra time off for travel. Also, she would spend time joining the nurses on their rounds and talking to them, getting to know them. But in the meantime, she wasn't writing up the management reports or updating the protocols, which indicate exactly what the nurses and doctors should be doing, such as how to give an injection. Plus the protocols indicate what to say to clients when they call about different things."

These protocols were particularly important because they were required by the various regulatory agencies and associations that supervised hospitals and clinics. So it was important to have these in place so that everyone on the staff would be consistently doing the same thing in providing patient treatment. And if not, the hospital was supposed to keep a report of that, too. Because of all the time that Vivian was spending being friendly and observing staff members, the reports and protocols weren't getting done. But Vince didn't know this, since he kept getting great feedback from other staffers about how much they loved Vivian and Vivian assured him that she was doing the reports and updates. Later, Vince discovered that she was only doing short one-page summaries, not the full accounts required.

Then, when Vince and his wife went on a vacation trip out of the country for two weeks, things got even worse. Vince left Vivian his credit card so she could handle any emergency purchases or payments to service vendors, such as ordering supplies for the hospital. But she used the card to buy lunches for all the staff members—two doctors, a dozen nurses, and a few techs and assistants—not just once, but a half-dozen times. She said she was treating the whole staff to celebrate her promotion. Of course, the staffers loved her for it, although Vince wasn't aware of this until a few weeks after his return when he got his credit card statements. In further checking her work, he discovered that the reports and protocols hadn't been done.

Although Vince was outraged, he wasn't sure what to do because the staffers loved Vivian so much and he feared undermining staff morale if he fired her. Vivian had done so much to create great staff morale, but it was at the expense of their productivity and getting essential work—the reports and protocols—done.

What Should Vince Do and Is There Anything He Might Have Done Differently?

Given the options—fire Vivian now or try to institute changes—what should Vince do? And is there anything Vince might have done differently to prevent the problems with Vivian that occurred? In Vince's place, what would you do and why? What do you think the outcomes of these different options would be? Here are some possibilities:

- ⮞ Fire Vivian now. She crossed the line in not only using your credit card to buy staff lunches, but also in telling the staffers that she was buying the lunches for them herself.
- ⮞ Have a long meeting with Vivian to go over the problems and explain that she has to change immediately or you will make changes yourself, including firing her.
- ⮞ Report Vivian's misuse of your credit card to the police, then fire her.
- ⮞ Spend more time observing Vivian on the job to decide what to do.
- ⮞ Talk to staffers one-on-one to find out what they think of Vivian. Tell them that you really paid for the lunches, not Vivian.
- ⮞ Have a staff meeting with Vivian present to discuss what Vivian did and didn't do and seek staff input to decide what to do.
- ⮞ Have a staff meeting without Vivian to discuss what Vivian has done wrong, including paying for everyone's lunch with your credit card, and seek staff input to decide what to do.
- ⮞ Other?

Here there are two major issues to deal with: (1) Vivian's actions and how to deal with them, and (2) the staff's misperception about Vivian's actions. In the beginning, Vince should have done more to monitor Vivian's performance and check that she was doing the necessary reports and protocols, rather than just relying on Vivian's assurances until she had first proved herself. Just because an employee is great in doing their job doesn't mean they will do well when promoted into management. Managing involves a whole different set of skills, particularly when someone is doing a person-to-person or technical job, such as Vivian was doing as a nurse.

While it may be great that a manager or supervisor is beloved by the staffers he or she manages, it is also critical that they are performing the other functions that go along with being in management, such as keeping the necessary records. Then, too, Vince might have provided Vivian with more specific written guidelines for when she was permitted to use his credit card. If something wasn't on the list, then she should check with him to get an authorization. This might have avoided Vivian's misuse of his card when he was out of town. Without clear guidelines, it's possible that she might have considered this an appropriate use to give staff members a perk. But it should be obvious that it wasn't appropriate for her to claim the credit herself for giving the staff members this extra treat—not to mention taking the staff out multiple times on Vince's card.

So what to do in the here and now? One issue is whether to fire Vivian. Perhaps if Vivian had just used his card once without claiming credit, and perhaps if Vivian had simply neglected to write the reports and protocols, Vince might try to work things out. He could take some time to go over her responsibilities and appropriate procedures, even writing them down so they are very clear. However, in this case, Vivian misused the card several times and misrepresented herself in claiming credit to gain staff appreciation. She also lied about preparing the reports and protocols, which she hadn't done at all.

Then, too, in ingratiating herself with the staffers, Vivian created a kind of "us versus them" relationship between the staff and Vince as head of the hospital. So under the circumstances, it is probably best to fire Vivian—and the misuse of the credit card could provide the perfect basis for this. In this case, that's what Vince did—he decided to let Vivian go. He quietly called her into his office at the end of her shift, explained the circumstances, told her she would be getting two weeks pay, and asked her to leave at once. This way, she wouldn't be able to spread dissension through the ranks by putting her own spin on the reason for her leaving the company.

The second issue is dealing with the staff to explain why you decided to fire Vivian. The best approach is to bring everything out in the open and correct the staff misperceptions about her. Since Vivian's actions affected the staff as a whole, it might be good to have a meeting with the entire staff, so that everyone understands what happened. Moreover, having one-on-one meetings might provoke concern, leaving staffers wondering just what you said to others in these meetings. At this group meeting, you should level with everyone about what Vivian did that led to her firing. She might have been a great, friendly manager to work for, but letting everyone think she was paying for the lunches when she was using your credit card to do it was dishonest. And she wasn't doing the critically important reports and protocols, which jeopardized the hospital with the various regulators and associations that supervised it. That's exactly what Vince finally did. The day after Vivian left, he had a staff meeting at which he explained what happened, and he found when he told the staff what Vivian had done—or not done—they realized they had been conned by Vivian, too. As Vince explained: "Once they realized the company had paid for the lunches, not Vivian, their opinion of her changed completely. They felt that she had betrayed them by making false claims, and they understood how her efforts to gain their friendship had been out of line at the expense of doing other important work for the company."

Today's Take-Aways

- ☑ Once an employee creates an "us versus them" situation between the company and the staff, you need to subtract that employee from the "us" as part of winning back everyone else's support.

- ☑ Just because an employee does a great job doing what he or she does doesn't mean he or she will make a great manager or supervisor.

- ☑ If an employee lets the new power of a promotion to management go to his or her head, you may have to cut off that head.

- ☑ If you have an employee who finds it more important to be adored by staff than to do the most important work, it may be time to show that employee the "dore"—whoops, door.

4

The Arrogant A**Hole

"Insufferable" might be a way to describe the person who is good, knows he or she is good, and repeatedly lets other people know all about it. This is a person who is arrogant, abrasive, and obnoxious with co-workers, and who sometimes bullies those beneath him or her on the totem pole, turning them into jelly or reducing them to tears. Why would a person continue to get away with this? Because they are so good at what they do and they literally frighten others into backing down or backing off.

That's the situation which Sam faced when he took over as sales manager for a furniture sales company with a half-dozen sales people and several administrative clerks. Davis was the star performer, both in getting leads and closing sales, and on average he sold more per customer than anyone else on the sales team. But he was a terror to work with in the office.

As Sam described it, "Davis would browbeat the administrative people. Sometimes he would leave the clerk-typist in tears, although the next day he would come in with a flower for her to try to make up. He was also very demanding. He would often change things. Once he made a clerk redo a whole flyer because he decided after giving his approval that he didn't like a particular picture. So he chose a larger one, and the whole layout had to be changed."

In a few cases, clerks left and went to other jobs, or they tried some quiet sabotage to get back at Davis for his treatment of them. For instance, they might misspell a few words in a proposal or put in the wrong pricing information. Or rather than finish a proposal Davis needed, they would go home without completing it. But Davis was able to talk his way out of any errors or missing information with customers, so he continued to have a great sales record.

Sometimes Davis also engaged in unethical or even illegal tactics that contributed to sales. For example, once he created an incentive program for customers that broke the company's rules.

"He set up a frequent buyer program, and then he was rebating commissions to the customers to build up his sales stats," Sam explained. "But that's against company policy, because it would end up reducing the commissions for everyone. The whole thing would have blown up in the company's face if we didn't put a stop to it."

Several times, Sam talked to Davis about his behavior, and each time Davis would agree to change. He would be nicer to the clerical staff, he promised. He would follow company policies. Then, within a few days, he would be back to his old form again. However, since he was the company's top salesman, Sam wasn't sure what to do.

What Should Sam Do?

In Sam's place, what would you do and why? What do you think the outcomes of these different options would be? Here are some possibilities for what to do:

⊃ Fire him even if he is the top salesman. No one likes him and he is creating too much havoc in the office with his arrogant behavior.

⊃ Talk to Davis one last time and tell him to either learn to treat others decently or you will fire him even if he is the top salesman.

⊃ Change Davis's territory so he has to struggle harder to make sales. If his sales decline, he may not be such an arrogant, a**hole.

⊃ Tell Davis he will have to do his own administrative work from now on because the clerical staff will no longer work with him.

➲ Have a meeting with the clerical staff people to let them know you are aware of the situation. Urge them not to take Davis's rude behavior personally, to just go along with him and not let him upset them.

➲ Other?

The big problem is trying to reconcile Davis's superior performance with the demeaning way he treats others in the company. While it might be ideal to fire Davis, bottom line considerations for the company mean that you have to look at the profit from his sales compared to any losses that may result from his arrogant behavior, such as clerical staff leaving. Should his behavior cross over the line into being abusive, then you'll have to watch out for potential litigation from an administrative aide for creating a hostile workplace environment. But if Davis is just being a jerk and upsetting people with his last-minute changes and insults about being inept, the possibility of a lawsuit is probably not a factor.

As for talking to Davis, unless you are going to follow up by firing him, giving him one last warning is probably a futile gesture, particularly since talking to him hasn't worked in the past.

It also might be counterproductive for the company's success to make it harder for Davis to sell successfully, as would be the case if you suddenly changed his territory. Perhaps you might tell Davis he will have to do his own administrative work in the future because the staff no longer wants to work with him, unless he can persuade the staffers otherwise. Davis might realize that he has to trade being nicer to staff in order to get work he wants done although he can, of course, always do it himself.

Alternatively, if this tactic seems like it could undermine sales, you might take steps to calm down people in the office by meeting with the staff to explain the situation and help them better cope with dealing with Davis's behavior. If everyone can openly agree that Davis is really behaving like a jerk, they may be better able to support each other in learning to deal with him and not get upset by his antics.

In Sam's case, the situation did go on for several years while Davis continued to rack up sales, and the staffers simply learned to not get upset by Davis's actions. In fact, they sometimes even joked about the latest Davis put-down or bad behavior, so that became the way that everyone learned to adjust.

But what finally changed Davis is that he had a huge sales failure, followed by several other defeats. The first sales blow-up occurred after he worked long and hard on a big sale and lost it. He repeatedly told everyone in the office that he would get this giant sale, lording it over the other sales people as well as the administrative staff. But he wasn't able to give the company enough of a discount, even by cutting his commission; when another company came in at a better price, they canceled the deal. That was followed by two more smaller but important lost sales. Davis was crushed by the losses. But his loss was the gain for the company staffers. As Sam described, "He became a decent person, and he started treating others decently. He was no longer the big cheese at the company and he knew it."

Today's Take-Aways

☑ If someone's doing a good job of being an arrogant a**hole, do a good job of not letting that person's behavior bother you.

☑ When a person is being arrogant and obnoxious because they are doing a good job, once the good job ends, they are likely to stop.

☑ Being humbled is a good antidote to arrogance, and if you aren't able to humble that person, it's a good chance that someone or something else will.

☑ Think of dealing with someone who is arrogant but doing a good job like a cost-benefit analysis: does the benefit of the person's good job performance outweigh the costs of his arrogant behavior? If so, keep the relationship going; if not, overboard with the S.O.B.

5 Cultural Chasm

Sometimes the basic problem is that an employee just can't fit into the culture with the rest of the employees, thus creating a tension in the office. The person may do a good job otherwise, but there just isn't a fit and the person isn't about to change. This is a problem that has been growing as the workplace gets more diverse. While the trend has been towards appreciation of diversity and making adjustments to get along, sometimes the chasm may seem unbridgeable.

That's the problem Alvin faced at his car repair shop. He had about a dozen employees, half of them working in the shop on the cars, half of them office employees including an office manager and others involved with sales, estimating, and administration. His employees came from a mix of backgrounds, including several Hispanics, an Asian-American, an Italian, and an African-American. And then there was Walter, one of the estimators. Walter was in his 50s and was from a fairly buttoned-up WASPy (White Anglo-Saxon Protestant) background. As Alvin described it, the environment at his shop was a place where "we work hard and we play hard; I try to make the work fun and joyful." So besides having occasional parties at work, most of the employees got together after work and on weekends to socialize.

But Walter was not part of this circle, although he was very diligent and methodical about his work. He knew how to write up a good estimate, was always on time, and generally made the perfect employee. But he just didn't fit in with the rest of the high-spirited, fun-loving group at work. Several times, when he looked particularly uncomfortable while people were joking together during lunch, Alvin told him to "relax more." But Walter didn't or couldn't relax, creating a feeling of tension for the others who were trying to enjoy themselves while Walter was hunched over his desk doing an estimate.

While the other employees tried to ignore Walter and just live and let live, tensions mounted. For example, several times he slapped down the estimate he was working on and stomped out of the office saying: "I can't take all this noise anymore. There's just too much for me to work." He also had a couple of run-ins with customers he felt were trying to cheat in getting their estimates for an insurance claim by claiming damage that had occurred long before the accident itself. Instead of saying something like, "If you can just tell me what happened, I'll pass it on to the insurance company," he would challenge the customer by asking such things as, "Well, why is the rust there, but not there?" The result was that some of these customers took their insurance work elsewhere. Sure, they had tried to inflate their claim if they could, but he could have just filed a report of what he had found without confronting the customer, leaving it up to the insurance company to decide.

Finally, an incident erupted with the office manager, Sheila. He snapped at her about how things were getting too noisy again and how she should run a more professional office so everyone could do better work. She snapped back that if he didn't like it, it was his problem. Walter then reported Sheila to Alvin, telling Alvin he should ask Sheila to leave. "But that's preposterous," Alvin responded. "She's been doing a great job. So if you have a personal issue with her, you should talk to her about it." But Walter never did because he was the kind of person who just kept his thoughts and feelings bottled up, and he was not one to apologize or back down himself.

Alvin agonized over what to do. Walter had been there for about a year and did good work. He was also 55, and Alvin was concerned that he would have trouble getting another job. Plus, his approach had been to be very supportive of his workers, helping them to work towards a good retirement or buy a house if they wanted one.

What Should Alvin Do Now and What Might He Have Done Differently?

So what should Alvin do now, and is there anything he might have done differently in the past? In Alvin's place, what would you do and why? What do you think the outcomes of these different options would be? Here are some possibilities:

⮕ Tell Walter he's got to leave because he isn't able to get along with the other employees. Don't feel guilty; his future is not your problem.

⮕ Find another room or build a small enclosed room where Walter can work in silence without having to mix with the other employees.

⮕ Buy Walter some ear muffs so he can tune out the other employees.

⮕ Have a long talk with Walter about how he has to change so he fits in better with the other employees. Give him two weeks to change or he has to go.

⮕ Suggest that Walter might be more comfortable at another car repair shop, and he might find one closer to where he lives so he would have a shorter commute. Then hope he takes the hint and leaves.

⮕ Have a meeting with everyone in the office so other employees can air their gripes about Walter and let him know what changes they want.

⮕ Other?

This is the kind of situation where it's best to act quickly to try to make changes early on, rather than let tensions continue to escalate. So initially, after a few weeks, Alvin probably should have had a long talk with Walter about how he needed to change rather than just casually urging him to relax more. And then, if he didn't adjust, it might have been better to tell him it wasn't working out because of the tensions in the office, even though he was doing a good job, rather than waiting for a year. In fact, that's what Alvin wished he had done, rather than letting the situation go on for so longer.

But that was then; this is now. Alvin might give Walter a final chance to change and explain why he has to develop a better relationship with others in the office. Since there is already tension between Walter and other employees, having everyone come together to share their gripes about Walter and tell him what changes they would like is probably not a good idea. Walter is someone who is closed off to others and has difficulty expressing his feelings, so such a meeting could easily turn ugly, making Walter even more angry as he feels a "them versus me" situation. Instead, a one-on-one meeting could be used to outline the changes you want Walter to make if he's willing, such as personally meeting with other employees with whom he has had particular conflicts, such as Sheila.

However, since the situation has already gone on for a year and Walter has continuously shown a prickly, unfriendly disposition, it is likely that such a meeting won't work. Thus, if he seems at all resistant, it's time to simply explain that you've been trying to improve his relationship with other employees for about a year now and it hasn't worked. He is creating continued tension in the workplace, so it's time for him to move on. Explain that you'll be glad to give him a good reference because he has done good work, but you feel he can't continue to work for you.

In making this decision, don't feel you have any obligation to help Walter prepare for his retirement or help him buy a house. These are really perks you like to provide to long-time employees, not anything that you owe to employees, especially to a relatively new one who isn't working out. As for finding a special room or building one, you really don't have to bend over backwards to make special arrangements to suit a single employee. The work he is doing is not highly unique or specialized, such as it might be if he was a creative idea person. You can easily find another estimator, just as Walter will probably be able to find another job. Whether he can or not, however, is not your responsibility.

In short, if you do give Walter another chance with a one-on-one meeting to explain why he has to change, keep his shot at another chance short—say, one to two weeks so if he misses, he's quickly out of the game. Or just drop him from the game now and explain why—he may be a good player, but just can't get along with the rest of the team. This was what Alvin decided to do.

Today's Take-Aways

- ☑ Sometimes the cultural differences are so great that an otherwise good employee just can't make it across the chasm.

- ☑ Just like in sports, if you have an employee who isn't going to make a good team player, you may have to let the employee go for the good of the team.

- ☑ As they say, try, try again—but after a reasonable number of tries, it can be trying to keep trying. So consider the trial over and make your decision: the job is terminated—case dismissed.

- ☑ In mountain climbing, if one member of the party is holding everyone back, it is better to let that person go early on before you all end up going off a cliff.

6

Negative Nelly or Ned

Some people are so negative, it's like a black cloud is always following them and they keep poking it to make rain. They are always looking for what's wrong, or what could go wrong in a situation, rather than appreciating what's going right. Such a person can be a real downer in the workplace, sowing the seeds of discouragement and undermining motivation. Certainly it's important to recognize flaws and consider the downside in assessing whether to take a risk. But the negative Nelly or Ned takes this critical approach to the extreme and is constantly whining and complaining. He or she often takes pride when a warned-of disaster comes to pass. Whether or not the person does good work, he or she is difficult to be around, creating an unpleasant atmosphere for other employees that makes it hard for them to be motivated or productive.

That's what Laurie had to contend with when she took over as a customer service manager for a software manufacturing company. One of the eight employees she supervised, Noreen, a woman in her mid-40s, was continually griping about what was wrong and pointing up problems in the way things were done—yet never suggesting any solutions. Moreover, not only was she getting the other customer service employees riled up, but she also had an ongoing war with the head of manufacturing. She repeatedly accused him of not understanding what she needed and not meeting her deadlines and priorities. Though Noreen was very intelligent and was often able to correctly point out what was wrong, she showed little interest in considering what to do about any of the problems. Her frequent negative input left others feeling upset and frustrated. She was often a polarizing and divisive force in the department when she triggered arguments between others over what to do about the situations she complained about—and about Noreen herself.

For example, sometimes she griped at staff meetings or on breaks to other employees about problems which had no effective solution. These problems were inherent in the software manufacturing industry, such as its volatility and changing demands, and the differing priorities for different orders. As Laurie pointed out, "You have to juggle your schedule and adjust production depending on quantities and who wants what when, so it's an exercise in compromise, which creates a certain amount of stress for everyone." But Noreen made things even more stressful by continually pointing out all the things that weren't done because of tight scheduling, such as not being able to respond to customer requests in time. So how could things be changed to accomplish these tasks more efficiently? On that, Noreen had nothing to say.

Several times soon after Laurie joined the company, she tried to talk to Noreen, telling her to be part of the solution if she pointed out problems and to be more a part of the team. But Noreen just gazed back at Laurie, like she didn't understand how Laurie could blame her for anything. "I don't have a problem. I'm just pointing out some problems that other people have." She didn't understand how her negative attitude could be a problem and considered herself blameless.

Looking back, Laurie wished she had sought to fire Noreen during her own honeymoon period when she was first hired and was given more leeway to reorganize the department. But when she did raise the issue to her peers in management—the controller, purchasing manager, and manufacturing manager—they expressed their concern that Noreen had a very important and difficult client, and she was the only one who could handle that client. So Laurie stopped pushing to fire Noreen, although she regretted the repeated turmoil in the customer service department as a result of Noreen's attitude. Finally, after a year, she felt she couldn't take the conflict anymore and left herself, not sure what more she could do to change the situation.

What Might Laurie Have Done Differently?

Though Laurie ultimately left feeling defeated, is there anything she might have done differently in the past to improve the situation in the customer service department? In Laurie's place, what would you do and why? What do you think the outcomes of these different options would be? Here are some possibilities:

➲ Fight harder with your peers to get them to agree that you can fire Noreen. Point out that she isn't irreplaceable, and her difficult client will get over her leaving and learn to work with someone else.

➲ Ignore or cut Noreen off at meetings when she starts complaining, and tell other customer service employees to do the same. Noreen has been glorying in the attention for her negative complaining; if you stop reinforcing that behavior, it will diminish and even stop.

➲ Since personal meetings with Noreen haven't worked, try outlining several specific times when she has been overly negative in a detailed memo to her and then discuss that.

➲ Have a staff meeting devoted to discussing why Noreen's behavior and attitude are upsetting people in the department.

➲ Learn to tune out Noreen's complaints when you are talking to her.

➲ Set up some motivational meetings with other staff members when Noreen isn't present to counteract Noreen's negative and divisive impact on the department.

➲ Create an incentive program to reward positive behavior; maybe Noreen will change her ways to get some of these rewards.

➲ Other?

It can be easy to fire an employee who is not only negative, but is also doing a bad job. But when the employee is doing a good job, especially when that job includes bottom line considerations such as working with an important customer, that makes it difficult. Thus, before firing Noreen, you should do what you can to overcome the problem or work around it, so her negative influence on the department is limited.

You'll find it's a good idea to seek a solution early on after you start a new management job. That's when people expect most of the changes and new policies to be instituted and people will be more ready to adjust. It's like a teacher setting the tone during the first few classes so students know what to expect. Otherwise, if you wait to do anything, people get settled into a routine; they already have created an image of who you are based on your first days on the job. Then you not only have to change systems and structures on the job, but also people's perceptions of you.

So what to do? You might try a multifaceted approach and see what works the best, if anything. Then, continue to do that. For example, a natural first step would be the one-on-one meeting with Noreen to go over her behavior and attitude that you want to correct. Explain why you have a problem with her only complaining about a problem. Tell her that if someone brings up something that is going wrong, then you also want to hear their thoughts about what to do to change the situation. Also, point out when her complaints have no solution, because that's the way the situation is, so she should learn to live with it.

But if that meeting docsn't work and Noreen is still casting her negative spell over the office, though she otherwise is doing good work, try some other approaches. One is to go from a more informal meeting to writing up a detailed memo, where you document when Noreen caused dissension in the department by being negative, and indicate what Noreen should do in the future to avoid engaging in divisive negative behavior.

Should the private meetings not work, then you might have a special staff meeting or set aside a major block of time in a regular staff meeting for everyone to discuss their concerns. Preface the meeting by saying the goal is to go from complaints and problems that people have to solutions for resolving the problems, so Noreen doesn't think that you have set up a "dump on Noreen" session. Rather, you are trying to illustrate a model of what you would like Noreen to do herself. Then, invite people in the department to share, and point out how you are trying to make Noreen aware of her negative behavior and how it is being received negatively by others so she can change.

Another possibility is to learn to tune out Noreen's complaints, just as she has tried to tune out your urgings to change, whether you are meeting with her privately or in a staff meeting. For example, if she starts griping to you, don't pay attention; then take control of the conversation and change the subject. If you are having a staff meeting, cut Noreen's complaints off early on by breaking into her griping and asking her to provide suggestions for what to do about the problem. Explain that otherwise you don't want to hear any more because you have a full agenda, and call on someone else. If Noreen is met with this consistent cut-off response, she may realize she needs to change if she is going to be heard by you or anyone else anymore.

You might also have a small staff meeting sans Noreen. Tell the other customer service staffers that you are hoping to change Noreen's disruptive behavior, and suggest other employees do the same to tune out what Noreen is saying whenever she is negative, change the subject, or cut the conversation short. This way, through classic conditioning techniques, you may be able to extinguish the behavior you don't want and encourage the behavior you do want.

Additionally, consider creating an incentive program that rewards positive behavior. Present this at a staff meeting, and point out that this is designed to help motivate people to do things that are positive and come up with solutions to problems in the company. And make the rewards enticing enough that everyone will want to participate, from offering extra vacation days off to trendy gifts and cash bonuses. Possibly, then Noreen will want to be more positive so she can get one of these attractive rewards, particularly after you and other employees have taken steps to discourage negative behavior.

In short, try a number of different approaches to see if anything works. However, if Noreen is still a problem after all this, make a stronger case for firing her with your peers. Remind them that nobody is irreplaceable. You are providing a product where anyone can offer supporting assistance on how to better use that product, so Noreen's difficult customer will agree to work with another customer service person. This CS rep is not offering a personal service where this personal attention is part of the product itself.

Thus, Laurie had a lot of possible ways to seek to modify Noreen's behavior. Unfortunately, she allowed Noreen's negativity and its effect on the department to wear her down until she couldn't take it any more.

Today's Take-Aways

☑ If an employee is always being negative, try to counter that with some positive magic of your own.

☑ Just like you can turn lemons into lemonade when you have a positive attitude, so may you be able to counter an employee bringing everyone down with techniques that bring everyone up.

☑ If an employee is getting attention when they complain, that may be providing them with the positive reinforcement they need to keep on being negative. Take away that reinforcement and maybe your negative reinforcement will stop their negative behavior.

7
Spilling the Beans

Another problem employee is the one who can't keep a secret and stirs up other employees with the information he or she shares. This lack of confidence can even become a legal or criminal matter when an employee breaches the confidence of customer records, such as when employees talk to outsiders about what's in the files. Even if they are talking to other staff members and not to outsiders, this can lead to serious problems when the information gets passed on and even more leaks develop—like a boat where the initial leak gets bigger and bigger until the boat goes down. But even breaching confidence on private personal communications with an employer can become a serious problem when it leads to misunderstandings that undermine the morale and productivity of other employees. And the problem is even worse when a once-warned employee continues to share.

An employee can feel a sense of power and prestige at having privileged information to give to others, a sense of control at being like a gatekeeper who decides who gets this information. Sometimes it can be a way of getting appreciation and feeling a sense of belonging, camaraderie, and closeness to the others with whom one is sharing information. And in some cases, it can be a form of indirectly protesting against management and company policies thought to be unfair by sharing information that puts the company in a bad light, such as telling employees what the company is paying to other employees.

That's the situation which Brent, the owner of a health club, encountered when one of his employees, Maggie, began talking about what she got paid and started asking others what they received. The revelations caused a lot of hard feelings as previously private information became public and led some employees to compare themselves to others. Some felt that they weren't getting enough in comparison. The problem began in the spring, soon after Brent gave a quarterly review and provided raises and certain other benefits to different employees. As Brent explained: "I have the two managers and other employees submit weekly reports on what they have done, along with any projects they are working on and what they have completed. Then, every three months, I go over these reports to get a sense of how well each employee is doing. If I think they aren't doing as well as they could, I talk to them about what to change; or if they are doing a good job, I'll tell that, too. If I feel the employee deserves it, I'll give a raise, which can depend on a number of factors—the employee's time on the job; their level of commitment; their performance; how much they improved since the last review; the leadership they exercised; and whether they achieved certain milestones, such as going to classes, seeing an executive coach, and so on. Then, if I feel they have done a good job and achieved these milestones, I'll give the employee a raise."

The system worked well for years, and Brent felt he was being an enlightened employer by giving the employees perks, such as paying for them to go to classes and get executive coaching. But then Maggie, who had previously been a good employee when she was running the gym area and leading exercise classes, began causing problems with other employees. Brent had promoted her to being a supervisor, which meant coordinating different health programs and classes given by other employees. Along with the promotion, Brent gave her a raise of about 15 percent over what she had been earning before.

However, after three months, Maggie said she didn't like being a supervisor; she really preferred overseeing the gym and leading classes herself, and she had had to cut back on those activities as a supervisor. So Brent agreed, but left her at the same increased salary level because he didn't feel he could take away the raise once given.

Three months later, although Brent was satisfied with her work, he didn't give her another raise. He felt he had already given her the raise he would have given her because he didn't take away the raise that came with the promotion.

Still, Maggie left the review session feeling upset, and she began to talk to other employees, airing her feelings about what she was paid and finding out what they earned and telling them she was sharing this information in confidence. When other employees actually told her what they earned, Maggie became upset, feeling she should be paid more given her many years with the company and the way Brent had repeatedly praised her work. In turn, some other employees began grumbling about what they received. After one complained to Brent, he realized what had happened and was furious, feeling not only that Maggie had betrayed their trust by talking about personal private information, but also that she had upset his relationship with all the employees. As he complained: "Now they think of the special perks we have given, like paid-for classes and coaching, as our way of paying them less with perks instead of cash. We started this as a personal development program for our employees; it's not instead of raises, it's in addition to—our gift to employees for performing well. But now they don't appreciate it as a gift, so we have to just stop doing that."

What to do now? Brent hesitated to fire Maggie, a long-time employee, because he was concerned the other employees might feel insecure about their own positions, thus creating even more turmoil. He also felt uncomfortable suddenly giving raises to other employees who were upset about making less now that they could compare their pay with others. Brent just wanted to straighten out the situation, but wasn't sure what to do.

What Should Brent Do?

Given the turmoil, Brent not only had to decide what to do about Maggie—should he fire her or not?—but also how to calm a volatile situation Maggie unleashed by revealing private compensation information. In Brent's place, what would you do and why? What do you think the outcomes of these different options would be? Here are some possibilities:

➲ Fire Maggie because she has stirred up the hornet's nest and the employees already feel upset and insecure whether she stays or goes.

➲ Have a meeting with the whole staff, including Maggie, so everyone can air their concerns.

➲ Have a meeting with the whole staff without Maggie being there, and ask for staff input on whether to fire Maggie.

➲ Have a one-on-one meeting with Maggie to discuss what she did and why it was wrong; then, if she is repentant, give her another chance.

➲ Change your office policies so your salaries, raises, and policies are transparent for everyone.

➲ Other?

This is a complex situation because Maggie has not only breached your trust in revealing private information, but also has created bitter feelings in making a normally concealed payment-and-reward system transparent. As a long-time employee, she has developed close relationships with other employees, making it not just a personal matter to fire her, but one that can affect the rest of the staff. The other employees have already been roiled by the revelations, which have, in effect, challenged your own way of running your business and opened up your decisions to employee input about the way things should be.

Thus, an important first step is reasserting your control so employees recognize that no matter what Maggie has revealed about your payments and policies, you are in charge. It is your decision how to compensate and reward your employees because they are working for *you*. Certainly, Maggie has been a valued employee in the past, but it would seem that she has undermined this value by the turmoil she has caused. And she did this in spite of your initial fairness in letting her keep a raise for a promotion to management after she chose to revert to her former non-management job. In fact, you might well have been within your rights to tell her that the raise was tied to the promotion and so taken it back. But if you didn't, you could have emphasized at the time how you were giving her this extra compensation. Then point up how you had already given her this extra amount at her next review so perhaps she might not have felt aggrieved, leading to her exposé of company payments.

But that was then, this is now. Maggie's behavior has literally poisoned the well, creating a sick office environment that needs to be healed. Under these circumstances, whatever Maggie's contribution in the past, it is probably best to let her go as smoothly and diplomatically as possible. Have a private meeting in which you gently explain what has happened and how much havoc it has caused, and pay her whatever is due plus any severance pay.

Then, to help the other employees feel more secure, you might have both one-on-one meetings and a group meeting with all the employees together. During the individual meetings, tell employees how you feel they are valued. Explain the rationale behind your payment policies and why you feel they must remain confidential between each employee. This way, you reassert that you are running the business at the same time you show your appreciation for each employee.

It might be good to then follow up with a meeting for the whole staff in which you explain why you had to terminate Maggie's employment, reassure everyone that you are not planning to fire anyone else, and reaffirm your policies for payments, reaching milestones, and rewards. Additionally, since Maggie has brought into question the value of the special rewards you are giving—like the classes and coaching—you might point up that these are extras to help employees grow on the job, not substitutes for monetary bonuses and raises. Then, continue your usual policy of having the three-month reviews, and have some follow-up staff meetings to let employees air any further concerns, discuss how you hope to address them, and reaffirm that while you want employee input, you will make the final decision.

Brent handled the problem in exactly the manner described above. Recognizing that Maggie had threatened the power balance, he let her go. Then, he held individual meetings and a group meeting and reasserted his own power. Gradually the seeds of dissension sowed by Maggie withered away.

Today's Take-Aways

☑ Once an employee poisons the well by stirring up other employees against you, you've got to get rid of the poison.

☑ It's your decision to choose what you want to be transparent and open in your business, not your employees'. So decide this yourself; don't let your employees do it for you.

☑ While it is good to listen to employee input, you should still rule the roost. Don't let your employees turn you into a cluck.

☑ If you have to terminate an employee for being a heel, you need to take time to heal with your other employees.

Part II

Incompetent

The Impossible Intern

Sometimes when you hire someone new to the world of work, he or she can seem like a grab bag of everything that could possibly be wrong about an employee. An employee who is just getting their feet wet often doesn't know how to control his or her everyday behavior to conform to the rigors and restrictions of the workplace. He or she may think that work is supposed to be fun, fun, fun, and while work certainly can be, the employee puts the fun part of the equation first and work becomes something of an afterthought. Pity the poor boss who is trying to help the employee learn on the job. Is this an impossible situation or is there a way out? After all, every one of us had our own first job at some point, too.

That's what happened to Douglas when he decided to participate in a community summer jobs program for high school seniors. He felt he would be doing a community service by helping a student with his or her first job in the workplace, while at the same time finding a low-cost employee to help out in his recently launched magazine publishing company. He felt as long as the intern could type reasonably well and write and format a simple business letter, he could train the student to do the rest.

So after reviewing a half-dozen resumes and having the candidates take short typing and writing tests, he decided to hire Cindy. He also felt this would be a good match because she indicated an interest in ultimately getting into the entertainment industry, while the other students put down future careers as teachers, a chemist, dentist, and a nurse. By comparison, an interest in entertainment seemed the best match for a job publishing a local lifestyle magazine.

Unfortunately, Douglas soon found that Cindy had an altogether different type of entertainment in mind. The first day, Douglas had Cindy type up some lists of advertising accounts, which went reasonably well. But on the second day, Cindy arrived with her iPod, and he discovered her typing as she listened on her earphones in her small office to the latest pop bands. Yet, because she seemed to be able to both type and listen, and she was working on her own, Douglas wanted to be the nice supportive boss. So he didn't say anything; he just gave her some additional lists to type.

Then, the next day, more warning signs appeared. This time, Cindy called in to say that she was having trouble with her car, so her mother would have to drive her to work. When she arrived about an hour late with a quick, "Sorry, but my mother had to do some errands on the way," Doug tried to be sympathetic and understanding. If Cindy wanted to stay a little later until her mother could pick her up, that would be fine.

Unfortunately, over the next few days, as Cindy had to depend on her mother or boyfriend, her daily hours began to shift all around. Douglas adjusted the number of hours he paid her for, trying to be accommodating and telling himself that she was just typing lists that could be done anytime.

But then even more problems developed. One time he heard her on her cellular phone, apparently talking to a friend about their plans for the night, and just as he came into her office, she put the phone away and went back to typing. So Douglas figured he didn't have to say anything and just gave her some more typing to do.

Then, when Douglas had some extra work to meet a deadline, he was encouraged when Cindy suggested that her boyfriend and a girlfriend could help out. When he interviewed her boyfriend, however, and asked him what experience he had, the boyfriend's remark—"Just chilling with my friends everyday"—wasn't encouraging. And when he interviewed her girlfriend, he found she could barely type or write a coherent English sentence. It was as if Cindy had no idea about what was required to hold a job in an office, even if she was a good typist and could write a reasonably good letter herself.

The final straw came when Douglas was closing down the computers for the day, soon after Cindy had left. He noticed an odd folder on the desktop that was marked "Cindy." When he opened it up, he discovered some photos of Cindy and her friends. Apparently, she had taken time at work to download photos she had developed and saved them on the computer.

If that was the first incident, Douglas might have simply said something to Cindy. But now, after a series of misfires, Douglas decided the situation had gone too far. He felt that Cindy didn't seem to have the right work ethic to do the job. Not only was her schedule frequently erratic, but she was increasingly doing non-work activities on the job—from chatting on the phone with her friends to downloading photos. Plus, she seemed to have no clue when she recommended other employees that the fact that they were her good friends was not good enough.

So that afternoon, Douglas called the community service organization that had arranged for Cindy's employment, told them that Cindy wasn't working out and why, and that was that. He felt relieved he didn't have to tell Cindy himself and face a possible blow-up, and he was glad that the community service worker seemed very understanding and eager to help him find another employee. He just hoped the next arrangement would work out better, or if not, maybe he should forget about trying to hire interns and just hire seasoned employees, even if he had to pay substantially more.

What Should Douglas Have Done?

While Douglas ultimately terminated Cindy's employment due to so many problems, perhaps he might have resolved the problem much sooner. In Douglas's place, what would you do and why? What do think the outcomes of these different options would be? Here are some possibilities:

- ⮑ Hire someone else in the first place. Someone interested in an entertainment career might be more interested in a glamour job; someone interested in a more serious career like being a chemist, nurse, or teacher might actually be a better fit for doing detailed work.

⮑ Monitor Cindy's work more closely in the first few days to make sure she is doing it right.

⮑ Give Cindy some clear guidelines about what is or isn't acceptable.

⮑ Don't try to be so nice. Be firm when Cindy is doing something wrong and don't let her get away with developing sloppy work habits.

⮑ Don't let Cindy listen to pop music on the job, even if it doesn't interfere with her typing. Explain to her that it doesn't create a proper work environment.

⮑ Other?

The basic problem here is that Douglas did not set clear enough limits from the get-go. He was the one who thought he would be helping someone out. Ignoring the person and offering no coaching or managing is not helpful. For one thing, he might have more clearly indicated to Cindy his expectations and what the job entailed so she had no illusions of the glamour associated with entertainment.

Also, even while Cindy might be a good typist and could work alone, he should have monitored her more closely in the beginning, checking that she was doing the right thing and was focused on the job.

Then, too, he shouldn't have let her repeatedly relax the hours of work and working conditions. While such options might work well with a more seasoned employee who has already shown he or she is able to thrive by working on his or her own, a new employee generally needs more guidelines and limits. Instead, Cindy may have gotten the impression that she could get away with things when Douglas was trying to be supportive and understanding. With a new young employee, in a sense, Douglas was stepping into the role of the parent. But was not providing enough discipline, leaving Cindy the opportunity to run wild, which is what she increasingly did.

For example, when Cindy had trouble getting to work due to car problems, Douglas might have made an exception once or twice; but then he should have told Cindy that she would have to make arrangements to get there on time if she wanted to keep the job. If her own car, mother, or boyfriend couldn't get her there in a timely fashion, there was always the bus. Likewise, when Douglas discovered Cindy making phone calls to friends on her cell phone, he should have done more than simply walking in and seeing her stop. Instead, he should have set the limits—no personal calls on the job, except perhaps for a short call to make arrangements for meeting someone for lunch or after work.

With someone new to the workforce, you really can't expect them to know much. And you can't be upset when they don't read your mind. By not setting limits and providing guidelines in the first place, Douglas most certainly contributed to Cindy becoming the impossible intern who was increasingly not doing the job and not respecting the usual conventions of the workplace. Douglas didn't teach her in his efforts to be too nice and supportive, so ultimately he had to let her go, although perhaps he might have confronted her himself to tell her why. And perhaps next time, Cindy might learn what it takes to be a good employee.

Today's Take Aways

- ☑ If you want an employee to follow your rules, clarify what those rules are in the first place.

- ☑ While it's nice to be nice, being too nice can let your employee think you are too easy.

- ☑ If you find an employee starting to take advantage of you, show them that you won't take it.

- ☑ While a fun environment can often contribute to greater worker productivity, it's time to end the recess if an employee is having too much fun at the expense of the job.

9

Damaged Goods

What can you do about the kind of employee who is a problem for everyone, who gets passed on from manager to manager? This sometimes happens because no one wants to be the bad guy who lets the employee go, particularly if there is a fear of legal repercussions due to employee protection legislation. So the employee can go on continually disrupting office activities, and frustrating managers for quite some time until pressures build even more to take some action. What action can you take?

That's the situation that Bethany, a bank manager, faced when Hilda, a problem sales employee in her early 40s, was transferred into her area. Ironically, Bethany had just arranged to have another difficult employee—who was constantly whining and complaining, and demoralizing other staff members—transferred into another department when the head of the bank decided to give her Hilda as a replacement. Why? Because as the bank president told her, "If you think you've been having problems with Alice (the employee who was being transferred), just wait until you meet Hilda." He said it jokingly, but Bethany felt that she was being set up because of the political nature of the bank. She was not one of the insiders and so she was the designated manager to deal with problems. Making this case more complicated was the fact that Hilda had a disability—she was suffering from the early symptoms of lupus. The condition led her joints to ache and she was often tired, but Bethany tried the best she could to work with Hilda.

Early on, Bethany had all sorts of problems with her new employee. One time Hilda left on a ten-minute break, but came back an hour-and-a-half later wearing bedroom slippers. Her excuse was that her shoes were uncomfortable and all she had at home were the slippers. Bethany responded by telling Hilda the slippers were inappropriate for the workplace and sent her home for the day. After that, the bank policies were firmed up to prohibit all employees from leaving the building during the short break times.

Hilda also had trouble getting along with other staffers. As Bethany complained: "She wanted extra support from the staffers, help doing her own work. She wanted them to file her new customer signature cards instead of filing them herself, and she wanted staffers to follow up with phone calls to prospects she interviewed." When Bethany told Hilda this work was her own responsibility, Hilda complained that bending down to do the filing hurt her back. Bethany arranged for her to have an ergonomically correct chair, but said she still had to do her own filing. While Hilda agreed to go along with this arrangement, she did it reluctantly.

Then another problem developed when Hilda attended the bank's weekly platform meetings, where the higher-ups discussed new programs and how to present them. While Hilda really enjoyed going to the meetings, she also asked a lot of questions and frequently expressed complaints, which proved distracting for the other employees. One new employee even complained about this. So Bethany's own manager came to her, telling her to tell Hilda she couldn't go to the meetings anymore. When Bethany told her this, Hilda burst into tears. "I really felt bad for her. She was so upset," Bethany said. But she felt she had little choice other than to tell Hilda what had been already decided.

At other times, Hilda simply went off on tirades, such as complaining that Bethany was hassling her too much in asking for her time card. She also spent an unusually long time on certain tasks, such as one time when she spent several hours cleaning out her desk. Sometimes, out of frustration, Bethany was a little abrupt with Hilda, such as saying, "Look, just get it done," when Hilda was griping about some task. A few times when Bethany apologized for being short with her, Hilda apologized herself, saying she was sorry for being so "bitchy."

Ultimately, though, Bethany got the word from HR that Hilda had to go. There were just too many problems, including repeated complaints from staffers filtering up to higher management. And it was Bethany's job to tell her, as well as ask her to write a letter apologizing for her bad behavior. Although Bethany felt uncomfortable telling Hilda top management's decision, she did and Hilda left. She never did write that letter of apology because she was soon in a disability program. But no one really cared. Everyone was just glad she was gone, although Bethany wondered if she might have been able to do anything early on to better deal with Hilda.

What Might Bethany Have Done Differently?

In Bethany's place, what would you do and why? What do you think the outcomes of these different options would be? Here are some possibilities:

⊃ Stand up to top management in the first place by pressing to hire your own employee rather than being stuck with Hilda.

⊃ Contact other managers and staffers who have issues with Hilda so you feel you have more support and don't have to confront her on your own.

⊃ Set up a meeting with Hilda and the other staffers in your office who have complained about problems with her. If Hilda realizes her behavior is a problem for everyone, this might inspire her to change it.

⊃ Combine your admonitions with a softer touch, so Hilda feels supported in your request for her to change her behavior.

⊃ Take more time to explain why Hilda can't engage in certain activities that are not in the employee guidelines, such as taking more than ten minutes for breaks or expecting staff members to do her paperwork for her.

⊃ Don't wait for directives from HR to fire Hilda; fire her yourself after a particularly egregious infraction.

⊃ Have a meeting with Hilda to give her feedback from other employees about what she is doing wrong, such as advising her not to complain and ask so many questions at staff meetings. That way, she might be able to change what she is doing in a timely fashion.

➲ Other?

In this case, Bethany knew she was getting a problem employee transferred to her department. If she couldn't stop the transfer, she might have done more to set the stage to let the employee know what was expected and show her willingness to help her do better. For example, Bethany might have set up a meeting with Hilda as soon as she was assigned to the department. She could diplomatically explain that she knew Hilda had had problems with staffers in other departments, but now she hoped to be able to deal with these issues to make it a better working experience for Hilda and the others in the department. Then she might have explained some of her expectations for the job, such as describing what tasks Hilda had to do herself and not expect support staffers to do, rather than waiting for this to become a problem when staffers complained.

Also, she might have gone over Hilda's limitations and found ways to work around them. For instance, instead of insisting that Hilda do her filing in lower level drawers, she might have rearranged the filing cabinets so Hilda wouldn't have to bend down low. In the case of breaks, Bethany might have explained policies to Hilda in advance and emphasized that if she felt she needed a longer break time, she should first clear it with Bethany and get an approval.

As soon as complaints surfaced about Hilda's behavior, such as her disruptive behavior at meetings, she might have immediately spoken to Hilda about this feedback. This would give Hilda a chance to change her behavior before she was prevented from doing something she really loved to do, such as continuing to go to these meetings.

Additionally, if there were continuing complaints from employees and Bethany's one-on-one meetings weren't working, she might set up a group meeting and frame it as an effort to improve relationships in the office. This would avoid having the meeting seem like a dump-on-Hilda session.

In short, Bethany might have taken a more proactive approach to lay out the expectations for the job and work with Hilda in a supportive way to deal with problem areas she already is aware of.

Then, if these proactive efforts aren't fruitful, rather than waiting for HR to decide that Hilda had to go due to recurring complaints, she might have taken action herself earlier on. She could give Hilda a clear warning that if things didn't change in the next week or two, she would have to let her go.

Today's Take-Aways

☑ If you are aware you have a problem employee on your hands, act proactively to deal with the problem before it gets any worse.

☑ Do what you can to help an employee with a problem, explaining what the employee needs to change and showing that you want to help support the employee in making those changes. But if the employee can't or won't change, it's time to change your own strategy and say goodbye.

☑ Besides trying to deal with a problem employee yourself, see if you can get support from others who similarly feel the employee is a problem. Present a united front in dealing with the problem openly, such as by having a group meeting with that employee.

☑ Keep careful records of how you deal with the problem employee, especially one who has a disability. If there should be any legal repercussions when you have to fire the employee, you are covered by showing why you weren't able to accommodate that employee and had no choice but to fire him or her.

10 Getting It Wrong

Employees can be well-meaning and eager to please, but if they don't have the right skills and claim they do, they can repeatedly make mistakes that can prove very costly. Sometimes, even with training, they don't have the right skill set or aptitude to do the job right—and they may be clueless to the fact that they don't have what it takes.

That's what happened when Elsie, who headed up a small carpet company, hired Gregory to be her assistant. Greg was an outgoing people person. Elsie met him in her building where he had a small crafts studio. He told her he was looking for more regular work because he had limited sales. She found him charming and personable, seemingly the perfect person to handle much of the customer interface. He just wasn't detail oriented when it came to keeping records or even getting customer orders right. However, since he had been running his own small crafts shop for several years, Elsie trusted Gregory when he told her he kept his own customer records.

But what kind of records? Soon Elsie found that he hadn't used a computer to keep his records, and even after she showed him how to use her computer, he didn't seem to get it. "I realized he often left out important information, such as the exact dimensions, and he made mistakes, such as not using capitals, in contract forms that would go to customers. In addition, he didn't seem to have a good memory for the different types of carpeting the company sold and what could be used where. One time he enthusiastically told a customer who was thinking of putting a bamboo floor in the bathroom, "Oh, sure, we can install that," when in fact, such flooring wouldn't be appropriate there. "His approach was we can do anything, so buy it now," Elsie said. "But that doesn't work if you are selling the customer the wrong product." Plus he spent too much time just chatting with customers and leaving other customers waiting, which reduced sales.

Elsie also found recurring problems when she tried to find other simple tasks that Gregory could do, such as marking samples. Though Gregory embarked on the task with enthusiasm, she found he often entered the code incorrectly, which disrupted her inventory system. She even tried reducing Gregory's hours so he would only work when she was there, but found she had to do too much directing and checking, which undermined her own productivity.

The situation went on for about a year. Why did she keep Gregory on for so long? Elsie pointed to a few offsets. "We were shorthanded, and he would go to trade shows for us where he was very outgoing and made good contacts." But ultimately, Gregory became more of a liability than a benefit. Around that time, Gregory decided to move his own craft business to another city, so the employment arrangement naturally ended. This was a conclusion which Elsie preferred, because she had found Gregory so well-intentioned and personable that she hated the thought of having to tell him he wasn't working out.

What Should Elsie Have Done Differently?

Elsie had plenty of time—in fact, too much time—to either try to arrive at a satisfactory working arrangement with Gregory or cut her losses much earlier than she did if she felt it wasn't working out. So was there anything Elsie might have done differently to prevent the problems with Gregory? In Elsie's place, what would you do and why? What do you think the outcomes of these different options would be? Here are some possibilities:

➲ Elsie should have done more to test out Gregory's skill set before hiring him or assigning him to do different tasks.

⊃ Elsie shouldn't have assumed that because Gregory owned his own small business and even kept records for it that he automatically had recordkeeping skills.

⊃ Elsie should have been more specific when she interviewed him about the different skills required, beyond telling him that he would be working as a salesperson and keeping track of leads and results.

⊃ Elsie should have checked more closely when she asked Gregory about his typing and he said, "It's great." She should have at least had him type something for a few minutes to show what he could do and how fast.

⊃ Elsie should have provided Gregory with more hands-on training, including role modeling, and then checked to make sure he knew what he was doing.

⊃ Elsie should have fired Gregory after a month if he didn't seem to have the right skills for the job. She shouldn't have continued to find other work for Gregory to do just to be nice.

⊃ Elsie should have been ready to advertise for another employee if Gregory wasn't working out and not use being short-handed as an excuse for keeping him on.

⊃ Other?

There are many options that Elsie might have pursued other than what she did. You should determine early on—within a few weeks—whether an employee has the requisite skills for doing the job. If not, the probationary, trial-and-error period shouldn't continue on for more than a month or two for most lower-level jobs. What Elsie did was get sucked in by Gregory's glowing personality, which led her to want to keep him around and resist giving him the negative news of "You're fired!" So she kept trying to find other work he might do. When he still wasn't able to do that work himself, she arranged her own schedule to give him more supervision and direction, although her original reason for hiring him was to not have to work such overly extensive hours herself. Moreover, she held off confronting him about how badly he was doing and terminating him, due to her feelings that Gregory was such a nice person. But you shouldn't let friendship or warm feelings toward someone stand in the way of making the right business decision to put someone on notice or let that person go.

In the beginning, Elsie also shouldn't have relied so much on what Gregory told her he did about keeping records for his own business and being a great typist. There was just too much room for differing definitions and understandings about what Elsie and Gregory meant about records and what constituted good typing skills. This would be particularly helpful since Gregory was only running a small crafts shop with few customers where he was the only employee; in contrast, Elsie's small carpeting store had a half-dozen employees selling and installing products. So Elsie could have tested him out by having him show her examples of his own records and typing, or she could have asked him to take a few minutes to enter some information in the template for a report or type a sample letter for her. She might have also asked him to follow up their informal interview in her building with a resume outlining his skills and previous job experiences, apart from working for himself.

Additionally, Elsie should have been much clearer in the beginning about what the job entailed by not only telling Gregory these specifics, but also by writing them down into a job description. That way, she could more carefully go over the required skills.

Then, after hiring Gregory, she should have more closely trained and supervised him in the beginning, ideally by doing some hands-on training where she could observe Gregory at work and give him feedback—good advice for anyone breaking in a new employee. Likewise, when Gregory initially made mistakes, she could have provided corrective training and more hands-on training and modeling.

Moreover, she might have made it clear in the beginning that she considered the first few weeks—say, the first three or four weeks—a trial period in which she could determine for herself through closer observation if Gregory and her company were a good match. She could check the legal requirements, if any, in her area for handling trial periods, which might make her feel more comfortable about firing Gregory even though he was such a personable, friendly guy.

Then, if despite all this initial caution in hiring followed by an initial training and probation period, Gregory still wasn't picking up the required skills for the job, she should have taken action. She shouldn't have been so accommodating in repeatedly adapting the job responsibilities to try to suit Gregory's skills, rather than seeing if Gregory's skills fit the desired responsibilities for the job. There comes a point when you recognize whether an employee's skills either fit the job or they don't; some people simply don't have certain skills and have great difficulty learning them. If that's the case, no matter how much you like someone, it's time to let them go—a service to both of you. You can find an employee better suited to your organization, while he or she finds a job that's a better fit. And unlike Elsie, you shouldn't make excuses for delaying the process of finding someone new. Elsie said she kept Gregory on because the company was short-handed and he was a nice guy who did some good things. But she could have easily looked for another employee, even while Gregory was still there, to have someone on hand for a smooth transition.

So if an employee isn't working out because he or she doesn't have the skills you need—and can't acquire them in a reasonable and timely manner—then it's time to say goodbye. Be as diplomatic and gentle as you can, but say goodbye. The faster, the better to make this determination, and then to arrange for the employee to go so you can refresh your company with someone who has the skills you need.

Today's Take-Aways

- ☑ Don't let a good-natured, personable employee turn you into a pushover; instead push back when it's time to say goodbye.

- ☑ If you have an employee who just doesn't get it, it's time for that employee to get a move on—and that means over and out.

- ☑ If you want to be sure an employee has the skill set you need for a job, you have to first determine what those needed skill sets are.

- ☑ Make sure you and a prospective employee are talking about the same thing when the employee tells you what he or she can do; using tests or role plays is one way to find out.

11

Friends Forever

What do you do if a relationship with a friend or family member leads to bringing them into your business, and then the person turns out to be either incompetent, poor at social relationships, or both? You feel a certain loyalty because of a longtime personal relationship, but the person turns out to be poison when it comes to the business. Usually, you would either get a toxic employee to change for the better or terminate the employment relationship. But it may not be so easy to just put on your business hat with a person who has been your friend for so long. On the other hand, you don't want to undermine the business either by having the employee make costly mistakes or turn customers away through outlandish behavior.

That's the situation Anthony faced in a business he had founded with a major contribution of inventory by Rodney years before. Their relationship started in high school, where both were big comic book fans. When they graduated, Rodney had accumulated a huge and valuable collection of about 20,000 comic books, while Anthony had a much smaller collection of a few hundred comics. When Rodney, then working part-time in a local variety store, told Anthony he was planning to sell the books and hoped to get about $500, Anthony, a budding entrepreneur, had another suggestion. Since some of the comics were quite valuable, he proposed, "Let's open a book store together," and so they did. Anthony gave Rodney a 15 percent ownership share and hired him as his first employee.

Soon after they opened, however, problems developed which continued over the years as the store expanded, thanks to Anthony's skillful management. Eventually Anthony had a half-dozen employees doing different tasks, including receiving deliveries and handling stock, processing orders and shipping to customers, managing the front desk and cash register, and organizing events for the local community, such as meet-and-greet with authors. The basic problem was that Rodney had difficulty knowing what to do or how to carry out a task properly unless he was given very specific step-by-step instructions that he could follow precisely. Plus Rodney had major problems in relating to customers, ranging from being too loud and rude, to being overly friendly and talkative with certain customers who weren't interested in talking.

Anthony rolled out a litany of examples. One time, Rodney didn't open the store as he was supposed to or call to say he wasn't opening it because he was sick. Four hours later, when Anthony arrived, he found the store closed, and spoke to Rodney on the phone, he explained that Rodney just couldn't do this. He should make every effort to open the store as scheduled because the business depended on it. If he really was too ill to come in, he should call so Anthony could make other arrangements and the business could open on time. An obvious and reasonable request, yet as Anthony found, with Rodney almost nothing was obvious or reasonable.

For example, Anthony found that he had to give Rodney absolutely precise instructions for even the simplest task or Rodney would get it wrong. "You assume that someone can make minor adaptations or changes naturally, but not Rodney. Once I told him to look for an icon on the computer screen to open up a program for managing our list of customers, but he couldn't find it and gave up. When I told him it was in the middle of the screen, he explained he was looking on the left side of the screen where he thought it should be—and this was just a 15" screen. I've also had problems with him not being able to find things in the store that should be simple to find. Unless they are exactly where I tell him to look, he doesn't find them. If I tell him to get something on the second shelf, but it's on the third shelf, he'll come back empty-handed. He doesn't see the big picture; he just tries to do the particular task he's assigned to do."

Although Anthony tried to talk to Rodney to get him to change, he found Rodney became defensive. "He says he's doing what I tell him to do, so it's my fault if I don't tell him correctly. I either have to do that, tell him what to do, or he won't do it. And he doesn't have any motivation or ambition to do better."

Anthony also had repeated problems in getting Rodney to properly relate to customers. For instance, when Anthony noticed that Rodney was sitting on a stool while waiting on customers, he told Rodney to stand up while waiting on them. Rodney interpreted this to mean only when he was taking their money and putting it in the cash register. So Anthony had to argue with Rodney about exactly what he wanted him to do before Rodney agreed to do it.

At other times, he found Rodney became overly clingy with customers, trying to tell them stories when they weren't interested in hearing them. Anthony gave an example: "Say he asks the customer whether he watches a certain television program, and the customer says no, I'm not interested in following that. Well, if Rodney has a story to tell about an interesting episode he has just seen, he'll go ahead and tell it, even though the customer has clearly said he's not interested. Then, if the customer walks off in the middle of the story, he'll follow to finish telling the story. And if the customer leaves, Rodney will say they're rude. I've tried to tell him he's the one who's being rude in telling the story, but he just doesn't get it."

Additionally, Anthony had problems when he assigned Rodney to work on a campaign to promote book readings in the store. He thought it would help Rodney to become more social, but Rodney delayed doing anything and kept finding different excuses until Anthony had to take over the project himself.

So why keep on such a dysfunctional employee for so long—a relationship that had gone on for nearly 15 years when I spoke to Anthony. Because of friendship and loyalty, and also because Anthony felt protective of his high school friend and felt he could trust him with anything. As Anthony explained, "He's been a real friend for so long, and I know he doesn't have any place to go. Though he's in his 40s now, he still lives with his mother. He doesn't even buy his own clothes, and I don't think anyone else would ever hire him.

Plus, I did start the business mostly with his collection, and he does own 15 percent of it. So that's why I haven't let him go."

Still, there were times where Rodney's involvement interfered with running the business. Could or should Anthony do anything to deal with this situation?

What Should Anthony Do?

In Anthony's place, what would you do and why? What do you think the outcomes of these different options would be? Here are some possibilities:

- ⮑ Buy out Rodney's share of the business and let him go. You've been putting friendship first for too long; there's no need to continue a dysfunctional relationship.

- ⮑ Let Rodney keep his 15 percent, but otherwise, hire another employee to do what Rodney is supposed to be doing and terminate Rodney as an employee.

- ⮑ Reduce Rodney's hours and assign him to very specific, routine tasks so he can contribute by doing what he knows how to do.

- ⮑ Adjust Rodney's hours so he is at the store only when you or another employee is there to supervise him.

- ⮑ Have a long conversation with Rodney, explaining how he has to change, including taking more initiative, and monitor his performance each day. Then, if you see any signs of changing, continue to support him with more conversations, plus some rewards for an improved performance. Otherwise, tell Rodney he has to go, although he can either keep or sell his percentage.

- ⮑ Other?

From a purely business perspective, the solution would seem obvious—terminate the business relationship with Rodney—both as an employee and, if possible, as a shareholder in the business. As diplomatically as possible, fire Rodney and work out an arrangement to buy out his shares in the business.

But in this case, there is a long friendship and a sense of loyalty to Rodney because his inventory helped to start the business in the first place. Plus Rodney has assorted personal problems, making him unemployable in most other businesses. And Anthony feels a strong bond with Rodney and an enduring trust in his honesty and loyalty to himself. As Anthony commented, "I would feel bad if I put him out, and he has nothing to do because I don't think anyone else would hire him."

In light of the ethical and moral concerns, it is probably best to continue to keep Rodney aboard, as Anthony has done. But at the same time, you should find ways to best make use of the abilities Rodney does have so his involvement is as helpful as possible for the business, and any potential for damage is reduced.

Since Rodney does well with very specific, routine tasks, provide him clear direction and break down tasks to keep things simple. Some examples might be assigning him to put labels on products, put boxes of inventory on specific shelves in the stockroom, and create an inventory list of products. Also, since Rodney is not effective with customers or in coordinating events, don't put him behind the cash register or in charge of a particular activity. And make sure you or someone else is around to supervise him.

That's essentially what Anthony did. He gave Rodney ten days off during a time when the store was especially busy, and he cut his schedule to three days during a time when there was very little traffic in the store. Also, with business expanding, Anthony hired someone else and he instructed that person to supervise Rodney by giving him very specific instructions and tasks to follow. Under other circumstances, Anthony might have saved himself the complications of continuing to deal with a problem employee. But in this case, he had to honor the long-time bonds of friendship, and he felt better about himself and the business by doing so.

Today's Take-Aways

- ☑ Sometimes it is personal, and it's not only about the business.
- ☑ If you feel you can't terminate a difficult employee due to personal commitments, find a way to work around his or her flaws and failings.
- ☑ While you may not be able to make a silk purse out of a sow's ear, you may be able to turn it into an attractive leather purse.
- ☑ If you feel you have to put friendship first, at least make the business a close second—or find a way to win at both.

Protected by the Big Boss

Sometimes politics rears its ugly head when you feel like you have to hire someone because your own boss wants you to, and then you have problems with that person. The person may be incompetent, lazy, a prima donna, whatever, but you feel your hands are tied because that person is protected by the boss above you. It's like that person has a patron behind him or her and you feel like you're caught in the middle. You have hired the employee, but in fact he or she answers to someone above you—the big boss who has the power to discipline or fire you.

That's the situation which Paula faced when she was hired to be a manager at a large consumer products company and one of the company vice presidents in charge of her division, Sherman, referred a personal friend, Priscilla, to her. Paula's job was overseeing manufacturing and production, and she had just started advertising for a project manager when Priscilla called her, saying that Sherman had told her about the job. So Paula interviewed her, although not as carefully as she did the other candidates who answered the ad, figuring that Priscilla came highly recommended. Plus, she was new on the job so she felt a certain pressure to hire Priscilla because she had been referred by her own boss.

But it turned out to be the biggest mistake she could have made. During the interview, Priscilla had claimed to have a number of skills, such as a proficiency in certain computer applications and experience managing other consumer projects. As it turned out, Priscilla had only a passing introduction to these programs, had trouble meeting deadlines, maintaining product quality, and meeting performance goals. Instead, where she shone was at parties and events, such as when the company put on sales parties to introduce its products to major buyers. As Paula observed and some other employees told her, Priscilla was clearly having a thing with the boss, Sherman. She acted coquettish and flirty when she was around him at the party, and Paula saw them laughing and joking around together several times.

So knowing about this relationship made it hard for Paula to admonish Priscilla about her poor performance and get her to improve. She felt she had no leverage to demand she do better or be fired, as Priscilla had the support of the senior VP. As Paula explained, "Since she knows my boss socially, it's hard for me to communicate with her about how she needs to improve her performance. We're a large company so we have formal performance reviews, but it has been hard for me to be honest and tough. When I did try to confront her about something she did wrong, she would talk back to me and say it's just not true, that I'm lying."

Paula also felt her position was made more difficult by the fact that it was hard to come back to Priscilla immediately with clear evidence of her poor performance. This would only show up when the product was finally introduced into the marketplace and failed. "So I didn't feel I had the firm basis to fire her since she had top level support, even though I knew she wasn't doing good work," Paula said. "And unfortunately, when her poor work was finally recognized, it would be too late."

So Paula felt stymied, stuck with a poorly performing employee yet not sure she could do anything about it because Priscilla had her own boss as her protector.

What Should Paula Do?

In Paula's place, what would you do and why? What do you think the outcomes of these different options would be? Here are some possibilities:

➲ Be firm and don't let Priscilla's relationship with your own boss affect your own judgment; treat her just like you would any other employee.

➲ If Priscilla is doing a poor job, tell her. If she says that isn't true, tell her that you are in charge and you are giving her an honest assessment of her work.

➲ Tell Priscilla you know about her relationship with Sherman, and you will take that information to Human Resources or the head of the company if she continues to stand up against you and doesn't take steps to improve her performance.

➲ Talk to Sherman and tell him that while you appreciate the referral, Priscilla is just not doing a good job, and it is affecting the company's bottom line. So you really need to find someone else to replace her.

➲ Go to Human Resources and explain the situation so they will support you in your effort to fire Priscilla.

➲ Go to the CEO of the company and explain that Sherman is having a relationship with Priscilla, and she is using that to keep her position even though her work is detrimental to the company.

➲ Keep careful records of all the times that Priscilla screws up so you can present this to her and Sherman as grounds for firing Priscilla. In the face of real evidence, he may not be so willing to shield Priscilla when you threaten to go to HR or the CEO if necessary about this situation.

➲ Other?

In this case, the situation may not be as hopeless as Paula seems to think. It is true that Priscilla has an advantage in having the backing of Paula's own boss because of their personal relationship. But if she can show him that she really isn't a suitable employee and her continued employment is harming the company's bottom line, he might well back off. After all, his own job could be jeopardized if he is pushing an ineffective and hard-to-get-along-with employee on the company because of this extracurricular relationship.

Thus, a good first step is to carefully document what Priscilla is doing wrong so you can present her with this as evidence. You don't have to wait for a formal performance review. Rather, after you have accumulated some documents for several weeks or a month or two, whatever is necessary to be convincing, talk to her firmly.

Then, if Priscilla continues to be insubordinate, you might approach Sherman to explain the situation. Mention that you are aware that he and Priscilla have a close personal relationship, but you hope he will understand that Priscilla has not been performing well in working for you. Perhaps he would be able to find another position for her within the company. Once confronted, he might in fact back down from backing Priscilla. He may not have been aware of how badly she has performed at work (he may simply be aware of her stellar performance at social events and, er, in other extracurricular activities). Whether he was aware or not, he may realize that he is now in an untenable position of trying to back someone for personal reasons ahead of the good of the company.

If you feel Sherman is unapproachable, it might be a good strategy to approach the HR manager and explain the whole situation. Then, HR may intervene and speak to Priscilla and/or Sherman and otherwise go to bat for you. Since this is a large company, it is probably best to contact HR and not try to involve the CEO in dealing with lower-level personnel matters.

Unfortunately, in this case, Paula wished she had taken some of these steps, but she ultimately left the company because she felt so trapped by the situation. She felt she had a job to do as a manager, but couldn't do it because she was forced to act contrary to what she felt best because of her employee's relationship with her own boss. Yet much of her problem was due to her own feeling that she was trapped, when in fact there were steps she could have taken to open up the trap and get out.

Today's Take-Aways

- ☑ If you think you are trapped because an employee is in a relationship with or supported by a higher up, you are.
- ☑ The first step to getting out of a trap you think you are in is to stop thinking you can't get out of the trap.
- ☑ One way you can break free of a trap is to open the door—and if you can't open it yourself, get some support for yourself.
- ☑ A good way to overcome the influence of a personal relationship is to put together some evidence showing that influence is not for the good of the company.

Last to Know

Sometimes a difficult employee can remain on the job for months because the other employees don't want to be the one to tell the boss and get that person fired. There is often a sense of bonding and camaraderie among employees, even when one employee is not pulling his or her own weight. The code against being an informant or tattletale can be so strong that no one says anything for weeks or months, until the situation becomes so bad that the employees finally decide to say something—or the boss realizes something is wrong and finally discovers the truth.

That's what happened when Bert set up a thriving construction company specializing in remodeling interiors and adding additions to houses, like porches, garages, patios, and extra rooms. From running a single-location operation, he had grown to having a team of seven employees whom he assigned to work on different short-term projects lasting from a few days to a few weeks. Typically, they would start off by meeting with him at headquarters, and then spread out to their assigned jobs.

One employee, Denny, turned out to be a problem, although Bert didn't know how serious this was for several months. Bert had originally hired Denny after meeting Denny's girlfriend at a business networking event, and she spoke glowingly of his skills. At their interview, Denny told Bert he had several years of experience on small building projects and knew the basics of construction, such as working with different tools and being able to do dry wall construction.

At first, Bert thought the only problem was that Denny would show up late, which meant the team would get to the job site late. "That reflects badly on me with the client," Bert said. Then Denny would be on time for a few weeks until he slipped again. However, usually he had some kind of reasonable explanation, such as having trouble with his car or getting stuck in traffic due to an accident on the freeway, so Bert let it go. One time Denny was four hours late, claiming car problems. Though Bert thought Denny could have easily called using his cell phone and could always leave a message, he thought at least Denny was doing a good job at work. So again, he gave Denny a pass.

However, Bert began to notice some problems when he stopped by one project site for a quick look at how things were going. He found there were problems with the quality of the work Denny was doing. "He would think something was good enough when it wasn't. Or he would realize something was not really right, and still keep working, resulting in the work having to be stripped out and redone. Sometimes he wouldn't get clarification on the work that was to be done; it would turn out to be more difficult than he expected, and he wouldn't do it right."

Bert also later found that Denny would take long breaks. Bert had a rule of no smoking in the house, so Denny would take a break to go outside, and he took more breaks and spent longer on each one than other employees. In addition, Denny would take credit for other people's work. This typically happened when Bert came onsite to check on the progress of the work. "After the work was done," Bert said, "while he was showing me around the site, he would say: 'I took care of this for you,' as if he did it himself."

For about five months, Bert didn't know about these problems. But then he came by a few times when Denny was taking a smoking break, and several times another worker said he had done some work which Denny had previously claimed he had done. So Bert began to ask the workers more questions, and gradually, and sometimes reluctantly, the truth came out. "I found out from the job leads—the guys in the field who I assigned to head up each team," Bert explained. "They told me that the workers were complaining about how much work Denny was doing, but no one had said anything to me because no one wanted to be the bad guy to get him fired."

So what to do? Initially, Bert had a conversation with Denny, telling him, "This has got to stop." He also explained that he was aware that Denny had previously worked on apartment clean-up projects that didn't have the same high quality standards. But now he had to do better work and be on time. At the same time, Bert spoke to the other workers, letting them know that he appreciated their work.

Despite Denny's assurances that he would do better, things came to a head after a drywall incident. Denny's job was to match the appearance of the drywall in another part of the house in a new addition. But even though he saw there wasn't a match, he kept on going, completing most of the room with the wrong drywalling material. The whole section had to be redone.

This time Bert was all set to fire him, but Denny begged for his job, saying times were tough and he was strapped for money. Bert relented, although he suspected nothing would change. And nothing did. So after two weeks, he typed up several pages of reasons, describing all of the complaints, issues, and previous conversations that hadn't worked, and he let Denny go.

After Denny left, he tried to get unemployment insurance on the grounds he had been laid off for a lack of work. Bert fought this because an approved claim would raise his own insurance, and Denny's claim was denied. The judge asked him why he had lied on his application for insurance and Denny said if he didn't lie, he wouldn't get the unemployment insurance. Oddly, while Bert and Denny were waiting to see the judge for a hearing, Denny asked Bert if he had any more work for him at that time. As Bert said, "He just didn't get it. He had this mindset where he was always looking for the angles rather than trying to do a good quality job."

What Should Bert Have Done Differently?

Denny was obviously an employee who should have been terminated much sooner. The situation dragged on for about seven months because Bert didn't have full information about how bad things were and because he tried to be a good guy in repeatedly giving Denny the benefit of the doubt. So what could Denny have done differently, and what might he do in the future to prevent a similar situation with a bad employee in the future? If you were in Bert's place, what would you do and why? What do you think the outcomes of these different options would be? Here are some possibilities:

- ⮑ Fire Denny as soon as you learned about his long smoking breaks and taking credit for others' work.
- ⮑ Give Denny a firm two-week, shape-up-or-ship-out ultimatum after you learn about the long breaks and credit claims, and then stick to that.
- ⮑ Set up a short probationary period of 30 to 60 days for Denny (or any new employee), where you provide extra supervision your-self and through job leaders. Then, if he isn't working out, let him go.
- ⮑ Don't let Denny's repeated excuses excuse bad behavior, such as being late. After one or two incidents, insist that Denny do it right or don't do it at all.
- ⮑ Interview Denny more carefully in the first place to determine what he really can do and don't hire him if he doesn't know enough about the basics of the job.
- ⮑ Designate the job leader as responsible for reporting on the per-formance of others on the project; then give rewards for being open and honest.
- ⮑ Other?

In this case, Bert should have been more critical in the initial hiring process to begin with. If he had, he would have seen the warning signs and wouldn't have hired Denny. In fact, after this incident, Bert did go through a more extensive hiring process in which he asked more questions during the interview about the kind of work the candidate had done, and the kind of places where the person had worked. For example, if someone worked for a friend or for an apartment clean-up job, that was a negative compared to someone who worked for a licensed contractor. Plus, he asked code questions to see if the candidate was up-to-date on applicable construction law, and asked if the candidate already owned certain tools and was thereby willing to invest in himself.

Bert should also have done more to check on references with previous employers, not just take a reference from a girlfriend who is certainly going to be biased. And he should have established a probationary period, which is exactly what he did for the future—setting up a 60-day period involving closer supervision and direction. Bert not only observed all new workers himself, but also asked for input from other employees because they had to work with the candidate. "So they should have more say in who they work with," Bert thought.

You should require other employees to give you honest feedback on how things are going on the project, particularly when it comes to the performance of new employees. Some may be reluctant to share information because of the stigma attached to being "an informant." Rather than entrusting the reporting task to everyone, make that a responsibility of the designated "job leader." He then has specific management tasks rather than just being another worker with some extra responsibilities for the job. And again, that's what Bert did following the problems with Denny.

With these added sources of input in place, you can more quickly get the information you need about how well other employees are doing. Therefore, you can take quicker action once you realize there is a problem. You should also not try to play Mr. Nice Guy (or Girl). Take action as soon as you feel an employee isn't working out—say, because he isn't doing his share of work, has a bad attitude problem, or lacks the work ethic to do a quality job. A single warning with a short follow-up to see if it worked is all you need. Perhaps give the errant employee one or two weeks to improve and show a commitment to change. However, if the arrangement is still not working at that point, end it immediately. Don't be a softie when a long-time problem employee tries to persuade you to keep him on because of his own personal problems. Remember, you're running a business, not a social service agency, and if the employee is interfering with your business, he or she should go.

Today's Take-Aways

☑ If you can't observe employees directly yourself, set up a system so you have someone designated to do this observing for you.

☑ Just because an employee needs a job doesn't mean you have to be the one to provide it if he or she isn't working out.

☑ It's fine to give a poorly performing employee the benefit of doubt once, or maybe even twice. But after that the employee should either be benefiting the business or it's time to stop giving any more benefits.

Part III

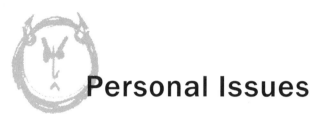

Personal Issues

The Sensitive Soul

Sometimes an employee can be very well-meaning and eager to help, yet be overly sensitive when it comes to taking any criticism. The employee just doesn't want to be wrong about anything and reacts to any negative criticism like taking a blow to the heart. This can make it difficult for you to give that employee any real feedback. The employee is like an eager-to-please vulnerable puppy, which leads you and others to bend over backwards to be protective so as to protect the poor puppy's feelings. This creates problems for you as the manager. How can you get work done properly if you can't correct mistakes? But this also can undermine productivity and morale when the employee really is making mistakes, and others try to work around them rather than upset the hypersensitive co-worker. In addition, other employees will feel they are being unfairly treated if they receive criticism and the sensitive soul receives none.

That's the situation which Gloria faced when she hired Allyson to be her administrative assistant. Allyson had recently returned to the workplace after taking a few years off to get married and start a family. But now that the youngest of her three children was entering kindergarten, she felt she could return to the workforce—especially since her insurance-broker husband said they needed the money. She interviewed for several jobs and was especially drawn to working for Gloria. Not only were the hours flexible, but she thought

Gloria seemed especially warm and supportive, which she was—a little like a nurturing earth mother. In turn, Gloria found Allyson's friendly openness especially appealing.

For the first week, everything seemed to go well, as Gloria explained what to do. As the week wore on, Allyson began to share a little about her kids and family when there was an opening. For example, during a cold snap, she commented on how her kids were all down with colds and she was glad she hadn't been affected so she could come to work. Another time she commented on how her husband was a gem: he was able to pick up the kids from day care and elementary school because he did a lot of driving to see clients. And she talked about the part-time classes she was taking to help her acquire additional business skills that she hoped would help her advance on the job. In turn, Gloria was a sympathetic listener, which encouraged Allyson to keep opening up.

Then, after the first week, Gloria noticed some tasks which Allyson might do more efficiently. However, as soon as Gloria began correcting what Allyson had been doing, Allyson got defensive and seemed upset, saying, "That's what I thought you wanted me to do." Gloria sought to explain that what Allyson had been doing was fine; this was just a better way. But Allyson seemed to think she had somehow disappointed Gloria and began apologizing: "I'm really sorry. I'll try to do better. I really will." When Gloria left, she felt drained, concerned about what she might have said or done that left Allyson feeling so hurt.

Later that week, she had other such encounters. For example, she asked Allyson to make some follow-up phone calls about new products because some of the people Allyson had called earlier that week hadn't returned her calls. Immediately, Allyson seemed to think that there was something wrong with the way she had made the calls, rather than recognizing that often prospects don't return sales calls. So again she began apologizing, saying she was so sorry that she hadn't been more persuasive when she first called and that she should have already followed through herself. And another time, Gloria pointed out how Allyson might arrange the chairs in a conference room a different way for meetings in the future. She had the impression that Allyson was especially nervous, maybe even holding back tears, as she outwardly smiled and said, "Of course, I'll be glad to do that."

Gloria wasn't sure what to do. On the one hand, Allyson did seem to be doing good work and showed an eagerness to do whatever Gloria wanted. But on the other hand, Gloria felt like she had to start walking on eggshells around Allyson to keep from upsetting her. As a result, Gloria started to feel very uncomfortable about giving Allyson instructions or corrections about anything.

What Should Gloria Do?

➲ Stop encouraging Allyson's stories about her personal experiences. The next time she starts, listen briefly, but then diplomatically steer the conversation back to business. Don't allow yourself to be drawn into a long, personal conversation.

➲ Fire Allyson because even if she is doing a good job, she is just too needy, which is making it uncomfortable to work with her—for you and others in the office.

➲ Assign a more experienced employee to Allyson to be her mentor and give her new guidelines and instructions. You'll feel more comfortable letting someone else deal with Allyson's sensitivities.

➲ Have a real heart-to-heart with Allyson. Tell her she is doing good work and that you aren't disappointed when you give her suggestions for changes, but she has to stop taking any criticism so personally.

➲ Send Allyson a memo, since you find it so difficult to talk to her, telling her not to take things personally. Explain how you like her work and that your suggestions for change are natural, so she needs to go with the flow and not get upset all the time.

In this case, a one-on-one discussion is in order, and as much as you might like to put your thoughts to paper or have another employee take the heat if Allyson gets upset during the conversation, it's best to do it yourself and in a private meeting in your office or hers. Your goal should be to be diplomatic, gentle, supportive, and understanding, yet firm in conveying your message. Since Allyson is so concerned about pleasing and gets upset when she thinks she isn't doing that, it's best to start with what she's doing right. Use this time to build her up and reassure her. Emphasize how valuable she is as an employee; how you appreciate her eagerness to learn, and so on. And then explain that you have to discuss something that is making you uncomfortable, but you are sure she can change.

With that supportive subtext, you are ready to get to your main message—you and others in the office need to be able to make corrections, without her getting upset and feeling she is doing anything wrong. Explain that you want to be understanding, but that she needs to understand that making adjustments and corrections are an ordinary part of doing business and an ordinary part of your job as a manager, so she shouldn't feel this is a cause for concern. And if she tries to apologize while you are trying to get her not to apologize, just ignore the apology and press on.

In short, use this meeting as a time for providing support, setting boundaries, outlining expectations, and making it clear that she needs to express less sensitivity in the workplace in everyday interactions. Even if she may be feeling upset by something, she needs to learn to control her feelings. Certainly, with other employees, who don't have this over-sensitivity problem, you want to encourage people to being open and honest in communicating with you, so you are aware of different attitudes, opinions, and feelings about how things are going. But with the sensitive soul, you want to encourage her to buckle up and button down, because she is overly emotional. Then, continue to support her work with frequent praise and don't let your fear of making her anxious keep you from offering constructive criticism in the future. Just continue with your policy of coupling corrections with some initial cheerleading.

Generally, this kind of reassurance should help to control any upset feelings. However, after awhile, if this doesn't work, consider talking to the sensitive soul about moving on, so she can find a setting where she will be more comfortable—and you will be more comfortable, too. This is what eventually happened with Allyson. She never got over her extreme sensitivity to criticism, despite Gloria's best efforts to help her, and Gloria finally had to recommend that Allyson find a new place to work.

Today's Take-Aways

☑ If an employee is overly sensitive to criticism and correction, be sensitive when you tell him or her to be less sensitive.

☑ Sometimes an employee can become super sensitive to criticism if he or she comes to think of you like a parent and starts telling you lots of personal information. If so, become the firm parent, giving support but also telling the employee firmly what you expect.

☑ Consider an employee's sensitivity like a protective barrier put up to ward off any negative criticism. So you have to get the employee to take down that barrier or you must find a way to helpfully dismantle it, so the employee can let criticism through and change accordingly.

One Problem After Another

How sympathetic should you be when an employee is going through a difficult time and has lots of problems? You may want to show compassion, but after awhile, you need to put the needs of the business first. As much as you may want to help, you can jeopardize the health of the business—or your own job—by taking on the role of mother, father, therapist, counselor, or whatever type of help the person is seeking. Moreover, providing too much help can serve to continue the cycle by locking the employee into a codependent relationship with you. The employee must strive to change and become more independent in order to overcome his or her problems, as well as help the business thrive.

That's the situation Vanessa, a manager of a company selling software, faced. She first had to deal with an ongoing war of words between two sales employees, Bonnie and Herman, and then discovered that Bonnie had a series of serious problems to deal with. Initially, Vanessa just thought the matter was a conflict about time and resources. Bonnie and Herman began screaming at each other over whose work the pool secretary should prepare first. While Bonnie claimed priority because she had gotten the work to the secretary first, Herman said he had an earlier deadline. So the fight raged on, and soon they were both yelling accusations and slurs at each other over previous projects. Then they were calling each other names and hurling character insults, as well as cursing each other. When Vanessa heard them screaming and sought to separate them, all she could think of was a playground with two five-year-olds fighting. She called them into her office to settle the problem and they both promised to desist in the future. From time to time, they continued to erupt into screams and shouts. However, as long as they only lasted a few minutes and gradually dissipated, Vanessa hoped the problem would resolve itself.

But while the office clashes stopped, they had a serious effect on Bonnie and, combined with other personal problems, threw her into a tailspin. The process started after one battle when Bonnie left early for the day, not wanting to fight any more with Herman, and after that, she called in sick for the next two weeks. After she returned, it seemed like her battle with Herman was calmed, although it was mainly because Bonnie literally threw in the towel and gave in.

Now, however, her other problems started to spill over into the office. For one thing, she was having difficulties with a boyfriend, and she was frequently on the phone talking to him. Vanessa overheard her on the phone several times and told her not to use the office phone for personal matters, so Bonnie brought in her cell phone. When Vanessa told her not to use the cell phone in the office, she went outside. In some cases, Bonnie missed staff meetings or came in late so she could call her boyfriend when he told her she should.

Additionally, Bonnie's mother, with whom she already had a poor relationship, became ill, generating even more calls, as well as yelling battles over the phone where her mother demanded Bonnie's help in caring for her. When Bonnie said she couldn't do it immediately, this triggered more angry calls from her mother.

At one point, Bonnie told Vanessa that things were getting so bad at home she would have to quit, and Vanessa accepted her resignation with relief. But the next day, Bonnie came to work. She told Vanessa she had changed her mind, and reluctantly, Vanessa let her come back. Why? "Because," Vanessa said, "she hadn't given her resignation in writing." Three weeks later, Bonnie said she had to quit again, and this time, Vanessa insisted she write out her formal resignation on the spot, which she did.

Looking back, Vanessa thought she might have handled the problems with Bonnie—which went on for about four months—

differently. She hoped to learn from what happened about what to
do if she had an employee with multiple personal problems again.

What Should Vanessa Have Done Differently and What Should She Do in the Future?

Vanessa definitely faced many different challenges as a result of Bonnie working for her. Bonnie's outside problems had completely overwhelmed her ability to handle her work tasks. In Vanessa's place, what would you do and why? What do you think the outcomes of these different options would be? Here are some possibilities:

- ➲ Once Bonnie and Herman began fighting, give them both an ultimatum to cut it off or you will fire them both.

- ➲ Tell Bonnie in no uncertain terms there are to be no personal phone calls at work, no matter what kind of phone, because she has abused the privilege.

- ➲ Counsel Bonnie on how to best deal with her abusive and controlling boyfriend.

- ➲ Let Bonnie use a private office for her phone calls with her boyfriend and her mother because she is having such difficulties at home, but don't pay her for the time spent making her calls.

- ➲ Tell Bonnie you feel very sympathetic about her personal problems, but you have to manage a successful business, so if she can't get things under control, she will have to leave.

- ➲ Once Bonnie has given you her verbal resignation, tell her it's too late to change her mind, and be prepared to fight her if she contests your decision to terminate her.

- ➲ Other?

In this case, as Vanessa herself acknowledged, you have to be firmer and put the needs of the business first. Sure, be supportive initially, but then draw the line. Insist that the person behave appropriately and leave their personal problems at home or you will have to terminate their employment. Remind yourself that you are managing a business, not providing counseling and therapy. If personal problems encroach on the office, as tough as it may be, you have to set clear boundaries for what is appropriate in the office and what the person has to resolve outside the office. You don't want to be a soft touch; people will take advantage of that to seek your support rather than providing the kind of performance for the business to thrive.

Vanessa explained the dilemma, recognizing what she had to do differently to effectively deal with employees with personal problems: "I know I was just too easy. For example, Bonnie always had excuses about her calls and said she needed to make them because of her problems. Well, I tend to listen to people. So I would feel bad for her. She was very insecure, because of her home life. She also had few friends and was very unhappy. I didn't want to upset her by making demands on her, so I didn't consider that her clients who were purchasing products from us might be unhappy. In fact, I didn't want to hear that. I just wanted to feel that if I gave her a break, things would work themselves out. But I should have fired her sooner, and I could have done so because we are an 'at will' company."

Then, too, besides firing Bonnie soon after her personal problems became a day-to-day problem, you might consider using some of these other alternatives that Vanessa suggested to provide Bonnie with some performance timelines to meet. You might accompany her on some of her sales calls to see how she is doing. If there are performance problems, provide some feedback on what she can do to improve; perhaps you might even give her a demonstration using yourself as a role model. Thus, with guidelines and some hands-on training, she would have a clear idea of what she had to do, in spite of her personal problems, to continue to survive and eventually thrive in the workplace. Moreover, if she failed to comply in a reasonable time (say one or two days) with your reasonable requests, such as to stop fighting with Herman and to not make calls in the office, you would have grounds for firing her. And if you already want to fire her and she resigns, there is no need to allow her to take back her resignation. You can simply terminate her yourself if she doesn't want to resign.

As for specifics, Vanessa provided a half-dozen steps she would have taken if she could have done it all again. "I should have put her on probation for two to three months where she could prove herself or not. Then, during this time, I would call a few of her clients or go to a few of her meetings with them to see how she performed.

Even if she was having personal problems at home, I would hold her more accountable instead of letting her get away with things. I would also look at the numbers of the sales she was bringing in to see if they compared favorably to the results of other salespeople. I would give her specific steps to complete while on probation, such as, 'I will make this many sales calls' and 'I will close this number of sales within a week or month.' I would require her to set goals and then work towards achieving them. I wouldn't let her say 'Poor Me! Poor Me!' I would have treated her special requests—such as to take calls from her boyfriend or mother—as something to be handled outside the office. It's like raising a kid; you have to learn to set limits. You have to learn to say 'No!' I was much too sympathetic. I tried too hard to be her friend. And in the business world, if you want to be successful for both yourself and your company, that approach just doesn't work."

Just as it was for Vanessa, so it should be for you. Learn to set boundaries and keep them so a person with problems keeps them out of the office and knows that if he or she wants to stay on the job, he or she has to perform.

Today's Take-Aways

☑ Don't be a pushover or someone with personal problems is sure to push you off.

☑ Create a boundary line in the office for handling personal problems; if someone crosses the line, help them to quickly get back on track.

☑ As much as you may want to help and feel sympathy, the office is not the place to provide the extended help that someone with personal problems needs.

☑ If someone you would like to fire chooses to resign, accept their resignation. If they try to take it back, you can still always fire them.

16

Too Much, Too Soon

Sometimes on paper, an employee can seem to have all the right stuff. But then, under the stress of a job with lots of tasks and responsibilities, they can't manage the multitasking and the stress. But rather than simply saying it's "too much, too soon" early on, they bumble along, trying to conceal the fact that the job is really too much for them to handle. As an employer, it may take you awhile to figure out the problem if they are good at concealing their inadequacies, even if they are not good at the job.

That's what happened to Edith, the director of a community hospital that not only served patients, but also put on an annual health fair with the help of a team of community volunteers. She hired Barbara to be a communications and PR manager, which included the responsibility for recruiting and coordinating the volunteers for the health fair. On paper, it looked like Barbara had all the right background, because she had previously set up some large events, and before that had handled sales for several companies in the health field.

At first, when Barbara was just writing press releases and the hospital newsletter, things seemed to go well. But once she added on the responsibility for recruiting volunteers for the fair, things started to go south. As Edith observed, "She would focus on one thing at a time and try to be a perfectionist about that. But there are a lot of pieces to the job, and if you spend too much time trying to get something like a press release exactly right, you shortchange yourself on having enough time to do something else."

Additionally, Edith began to notice other failings. Barbara had originally said she was good at sales, and she had listed three sales jobs on her resume to show this. But Edith noticed that Barbara was slow at setting up meetings with companies to sell the program to recruits, and when Edith accompanied her on some of her sales calls, she found Barbara was disorganized. "She didn't figure out what she needed to do in advance, and seemed nervous around people at the meetings. She seemed more comfortable working at her desk."

Then, Barbara began to call sick a lot, using up her two weeks of sick leave within a few months on the job.

The kicker came when Barbara had scheduled a meeting for recruits, where she would be speaking along with the community organizer who helped her set up the meeting with about 50 leaders of different organizations who might provide volunteers for the fair. So it was a very important meeting and she would be the main presenter, speaking about the program on behalf of the hospital. Then, a week before the program, she sent an e-mail to Edith and the leaders of the different organizations saying she couldn't go and speak at the event because something had come up for that night.

Not go? Edith and others at the hospital felt a sense of panic because Barbara was supposed to be in control of everything for the meeting; now she had suddenly pulled out, leaving everyone in the lurch, and using an e-mail rather than a phone call to explain. So what could be so important? Edith immediately called Barbara, who nervously explained how she felt this was a hard job, and she felt she needed to unwind from all the stress so she decided to go to a yoga and dance class that night. "What?" Edith exploded, to which Barbara replied, "You always talk about having a work-life balance. So I felt I should do this to get some more balance in my life."

Edith couldn't believe what Barbara was telling her. "If you told people three weeks ago about this class, it would be different," Edith said. "You could have changed the meeting date or the speaking arrangements. So now this isn't a work-life balance. Doing something like this is totally irresponsible and will set you back on your career path." Then, Edith insisted that Barbara simply could not go to her class, and Barbara did go to the meeting. However, she was not well-prepared for it. Since she assumed she wouldn't be going, she hadn't gone over the material and had only that afternoon to review her notes. Plus, she was so frazzled, she left all her handouts at the office. Although the meeting was only one town away and she could have called to have someone bring over the material, she didn't do that. Instead, she called a friend to read her as much of the basic information as possible over the phone and she jotted it down on some crumpled notes.

The result was that, even though she gave the presentation, she was very nervous because she wasn't on top of the information and she came across badly. "She couldn't fake her way through it," Edith said. "And when I got feedback about the meeting the next day, it wasn't good."

To follow up, Edith asked Barbara to send a personalized memo along with the handouts to each of the people who had been at the meeting, but it took her a few weeks to do that. As a result, Edith put her on probation. A week later, she gave her notice, saying that she realized it wasn't the right job for her and she just couldn't do it. Meanwhile, Edith had to scramble around doing follow-up and recruitment herself for a few weeks until she could find someone else to take over Barbara's job.

What Could Barbara Have Done Differently and What Should She Do in the Future?

Was there anything that Edith might have done differently, knowing that this was a high-stress job with many responsibilities? In Edith's place, what would you do and why? What do you think the outcomes of these different options would be? Here are some possibilities:

➲ Have Barbara do the job for a day, and include a sampling of all the different tasks she will be doing, not just a couple of tasks.

➲ Give Barbara some typical scenarios she is likely to encounter and ask her how she would deal with each one if it came up on the job.

➲ More critically evaluate the match between what Barbara did in the past and what you want her to do, given that there is a difference between putting on large events with some family members and friends and recruiting volunteers to help put on an event.

➲ Provide Barbara some more hands-on training, including role modeling, to show her exactly what to do.

➲ Have Barbara put on some recruitment meetings for you or others in the organization to help her prepare to give a good presentation.

➲ Give Barbara advance guidelines about what employees might do to improve their work-life balance and what is not acceptable.

➲ Help Barbara set up an organizational system so she can better prioritize the different tasks she has to do.

➲ Invite Barbara to feel free to come to you early on if she feels overly stressed on what you know is a complex, high-stress job so you can help her better deal with the stress.

➲ Cut your losses early on. Once you see that Barbara is having trouble handling all the aspects of the job, let her go.

➲ Other?

Since Edith knew this was going to be a complex, multi-tasking job, she should have spent more time in the initial interviewing process to make sure that Barbara fully understood the complexities and responsibility of the job—and should do likewise in future hires. She should have given less weight to Barbara's academic background and personal references and also recognized that it is very different to put on an event oneself with family and friends than it is to recruit a team of volunteers to do the work. While putting on the event may take organizational and event planning skills, recruiting volunteers also requires not only sales skills but the ability to speak at and facilitate a meeting. Thus, Edith should have looked for those skills, too. To determine Barbara's abilities without a proven track record in these keys areas, she might have asked Barbara to perform key tasks for a few hours or a day, either on a paid or unpaid basis depending on the time involved, to see how she performed.

Furthermore, to see her flexibility and versatility in responding to different situations, Edith could have given her some sample scenarios about possible situations she might encounter and see how she would respond. For example, how would she handle a secretary asking questions about what this event was all about before she would refer the request on to her boss? By asking additional questions and setting up scenarios and hands-on situations, Edith would get a better picture of how Barbara would respond on the job and whether she would be suitable for the work at hand. At the same time, Barbara would get a better picture of the many tasks involved, so she could better determine if she was really up to the job before taking it on.

After hiring Barbara or anyone else for the job, Edith might have provided more training by overseeing Barbara as she performed various tasks, such as setting up meetings or putting on a program for organizational leaders or prospective volunteers. Edith could then provide some real-time feedback about how she did. It would also be helpful to get ongoing reports from Barbara about what she was doing. Then if Edith noticed any problems, such as tasks that weren't getting done because Barbara was doing other things, she could help Barbara in better prioritizing what needed to be done.

Additionally, an open-door policy might help Barbara feel better, should she be feeling unsure or stressed about the many tasks involved in the job. However, while encouraging an employee to find a balance between their work and personal life might be helpful, it is not necessary to spell this out. Certainly, an employee should recognize that it is inappropriate to cancel their participation in a very important meeting at the last minute, using the idea of creating a better work-life balance as an excuse.

Edith might have noticed that Barbara was having such problems much sooner so she could terminate Barbara's employment much sooner. In fact, she might have put Barbara on probation in the beginning of her employment, rather than after five months when Barbara was struggling over sending out personal e-mails with handouts because she had done so poorly at the meeting. And she certainly might have fired her immediately after the meeting fiasco, rather than giving her another few weeks to mend fences. Not only did Barbara try to get out of the meeting at the last minute for a completely inappropriate reason, but then she performed so badly at the meeting itself.

Today's Take-Aways

- ☑ If someone isn't up to a job, find out sooner rather than later.

- ☑ If you know a job is highly complex and stressful, make this it clear to any prospective employees so they know what they are getting into and can better assess if they can handle it.

- ☑ Besides looking at resumes and references, try using scenarios and hands-on experiences to determine if someone is right for a really tough job.

- ☑ Provide training early on to help someone know what to do and how to prioritize in a job that has lots of tasks.

- ☑ Use a probationary period in the beginning, not at the end, to determine if someone is up to a complex, high-stress job.

- ☑ If an employee can't take the heat on a job that's hard to handle, turn off the heat and pull the employee out of the fire—a simple "You're fired" early on should do the trick.

17 Got Drugs?

When a long-time employee turns to drugs it can present a difficult problem. It becomes even more complicated if the employee is stealing the drugs, too—especially when he or she is stealing them from you. Should it be treated as a medical or psychological problem? A crime? Should the employee be helped, turned over to law enforcement, fired, suspended, or what?

That's the problem Natalee faced as the director of a medical center when she discovered that a long-time and well-respected doctor, Warren, had a drug problem and had been stealing drugs from the center's supply cabinet for his own use. The drugs were a combination of amphetamines and sedatives, and apparently Warren had become addicted to the uppers to gain more energy, and then used the sedatives to calm down.

Natalee found out when a couple of nurses came to her, reporting their suspicions that Warren might have a drug problem. The nurses had observed some odd behavior by Warren. He sometimes fell asleep at his desk, was late to work, sometimes wore the same clothes he had worn the day before, and was increasingly late in getting his paperwork turned in to the administration division. In addition, a few months earlier he had started to distance himself from other doctors at the center, such as by going in to his office and closing the door on breaks between seeing patients, rather than chatting with other doctors in the staff room. And he seemed unusually reserved and distant from the nurses, too, whereas before he had been very friendly and chatty.

When Natalee called Warren into her office and asked him if he was having a problem with drugs, he said he had lupus and that his medications were making him tired. But then Natalee heard from some doctors that some of the drugs they prescribed to patients were missing from the center's pharmacy, and after some further investigation, she discovered that Warren had obtained the key to the pharmacy and had been taking drugs from it.

The news came as a real shock because Warren had been with the center for about ten years, starting soon after it was founded. Patients came to the center on a drop-in or appointment basis and were then assigned to different doctors. They might request to see a particular doctor if available, and Warren was quite popular with the patients. Natalee was relieved to know that this drug use hadn't affected Warren's ability to deal with patients, which had always been one of his strong points. But now she had to decide what to do about Warren's continued employment with the center.

What Should Natalee Do?

In Natalee's place, what would you do and why? What do you think the outcomes of these different options would be? Here are some possibilities:

- ⊃ Call the police since Warren has been stealing drugs—a serious crime, even if he has been with the center for ten years.

- ⊃ Fire Warren immediately for both using drugs and stealing them, but don't call the police because this will be bad publicity for the center.

- ⊃ Put Warren on suspension for several months and tell him to get help. After that, you will consider possibly reinstating him if he can show he has resolved his problem.

- ⊃ Ask Warren to see a drug counselor you know, and suspend him while he is treated; then rehire him when he has resolved his problem.

➲ Permit Warren to stay on, as long as he joins a drug treatment program and reimburses the center for the drugs he took.

➲ Suspend Warren and offer to hire him back once he has overcome his addiction through treatment and reimbursed the center for the drugs he took.

➲ Fire Warren and ask him to reimburse the center for the drugs he took in return for your not reporting the matter to the police.

➲ Other?

It can be a very heartbreaking decision when you have to deal with a long-time employee who has a drug problem, but you have to put the good of the company and your clients—in this case, the patients—first. So you do have to end Warren's work at the center for as long as he has a drug problem. While he has so far been able to function with patients, a drug problem increases the risk that at some point he won't be able to do so. This subjects you to liability risks, which are even greater once you know of his impairment. However, since Warren has been a long-time employee, you might give him a chance to clean up his problem by either suspending him until he has overcome his addiction, or terminating him with an understanding that you will rehire him once this addiction is overcome. Additionally, you might make reimbursing the center for the stolen drugs a condition for reinstating or rehiring him. You might also do what you can to provide Warren with leads to a drug treatment program or counselor.

Even though Warren has stolen drugs from the center, it is probably best not to involve law enforcement. Warren has previously been a good, long-term employee who has developed a serious problem, so you may want to cut him some slack. Plus, this kind of report—a doctor who is a drug addict stealing drugs from the medical center where he works—is likely to get media attention, and that could be bad for the center's reputation. So it is best to handle this as a medical or psychological problem, which is best for both helping Warren recover and keeping the center out of the news.

In this case, Natalee suspended Warren while he attended a six-week rehab program. She also required him to reimburse the center for the drugs he had stolen, and after he got clean, she gave him his old job back, deducting some of the money he owed the center from these funds. Eventually, he overcame his problems and became a valued member of the center's staff once again.

Today's Take-Aways

☑ When an employee has a drug problem, think about what is best for your organization and your customers when you decide what to do.

☑ Helping your employee overcome his or her drug problem can help your employee, too.

☑ Just because your employee has committed a crime in stealing or possessing drugs, it doesn't mean you have to treat this as a criminal matter.

☑ Sometimes a second chance is just what an employee with a drug problem needs, and that might be best for your company, too.

☑ A first step in dealing with an employee with a drug problem is to stop the employee from working with your clients or customers. Then you can decide what's best to do —from firing or suspending the employee, to rehiring or reinstating the employee after the drug problem is solved.

18 In the Drink

Drinking can cause workplace problems, such as tardiness, missed work, and mistakes on the job, but it also can lead to accidents that can not only hurt the employee but also the business. When workers' compensation claims and costs are factored in, drinking can be even more costly. This kind of situation can be especially troublesome when the employee's drinking can't be proved but you know there is a problem.

That's the problem Judy, a staffing manager for an employment service, faced when she learned that Garrett, one of the employees she sent out on a job, might have a drinking problem. Her company handled a range of employees. They would find the appropriate employee for a client, but they remained the official employer, keeping records and handling payments for the hours the employee worked wherever assigned.

Garrett had been placed as a warehouse worker for a manufacturing company. The first month everything was fine, but the second month, Garrett began to have problems. He called in late several times, he had to leave early sometimes, and a few times, he arrived around lunch time with an excuse for why he was late—his car broke down, he had to fix a flat tire for the woman next door, he had to take a sick child to the hospital, etc. In Judy's experience, these could all be signs of a drinking problem, although there was no direct evidence that Garrett had been drinking.

Then, one day shortly after lunch, Garrett had an accident in which he hit his head on a rolling door. He claimed that someone on the other side of the door was pulling it down when he turned and the door hit him. His supervisor, Colin, thought that Garrett had been drinking at lunch and fell into the door. Colin immediately called Judy to report the incident. She immediately filed a workers' comp claim and had Garrett go to see a doctor. She explained, "We have to take these claims seriously and also check if alcohol or drugs are involved. If they are, any accident is the employee's responsibility, so no one has to pay the claim. If they aren't, then the employer—in this case us—has to pay the claim."

The check-up showed that Garrett had suffered a slight bump on the head with no sign of a concussion, and he was cleared to go back to work. Garrett also passed the alcohol and drug test, which meant that Judy's company would be liable for the claim unless a further investigation showed he had been drinking or taking drugs. However, Garrett didn't take the test until a couple of hours after the accident. While it showed no high level of alcohol or drugs in his system at that time, they might have been at a higher than acceptable level at the time of the accident.

So Judy wasn't sure whether Garrett had a drinking problem that may have contributed to the accident, and she wasn't sure what to do about placing Garrett in jobs in the future.

What Should Judy Do?

In Judy's place, what would you do and why? What do you think the outcomes of these different options would be? Here are some possibilities:

- ➲ Challenge the workers' comp claim, knowing that a further investigation will show that Garrett was drinking on the job.

- ➲ Call Garrett's supervisor at the manufacturing company and ask him to monitor Garrett's behavior to help determine if Garrett does have a drinking problem.

⮩ Have a conversation with Garrett about how you think he may be having a problem with drinking or drugs and you want to help him get over it, if this is the case.

⮩ Pay any claim and let Garrett finish out his current job, as you would with any employee you place. But then don't send Garrett out for any more jobs because you don't want to place an employee with a possible drinking or drug problem.

⮩ Other?

If you suspect someone may have a drinking or drug problem, what to do depends on your relationship with that employee, how long that employee has been on the job, and what evidence you have. If Garrett had been a long-time regular employee, it might have been worth having a conversation with him about your concerns. Show him that you are receptive to what he tells you without penalizing him and will hold what he says in confidence, and explain that you want to help him beat the problem. Some companies even have special alcohol and drug programs or outside resources to which they can make a referral.

But in this case, Garrett is an outside employee who has only been working for you two months, and it appears that the problem developed in the second month. You might want to continue to monitor the situation by getting feedback from his supervisor. You can then use that information as a basis for deciding whether to try to place Garrett in another position after he finishes his assignment at the manufacturing company. If you continue to suspect a drinking or drug problem based on what the supervisors says—citing continuing problems with lateness, no shows and excuses, or if there have been any more accidents—finish up your current employment contract and don't hire him out again. Meanwhile, go ahead and process his workers' comp claim as if he were not at fault for the accident because of drinking or doing drugs because you just don't have the evidence to show if he was.

And in this case, that's what Judy did. She continued to get feedback from the supervisor, and soon after, Garrett left the job. He never did follow through with the needed paperwork for his claim, so he never did get workers' comp. Why not? Judy believes it was because, "He really did have a drinking problem, didn't want to

admit it, and so he left. Knowing he was guilty of having this problem, he didn't pursue his claim."

Today's Take-Aways

☑ If an employee's behavior suddenly changes, such that a reliable
employee becomes unreliable, you may have a drinking or drug
problem on your hands.

☑ Once you think an employee has a drinking or drug problem
monitor the situation—or have that employee's supervisor monitor it for you—so you can determine what's going on.

☑ Just like with driving, drinking or drugs and work don't mix; so
once you feel a drug problem is likely, don't let the employee
behind the "wheel."

☑ Factor in a number of considerations in deciding what to do
about an employee grounded due to drugs or drinking—time on
the job, the type of work, whether the employee admits the problem and wants help—in deciding whether to fire or help the employee.

Sick and Tired

When employees call in sick a lot, it could be for many different reasons. They really are sick, or possibly they don't like the job, are bored, have something more interesting to do, or are looking for another job. The person could also be a hypochondriac who sees illness almost everywhere or magnifies small, inconsequential symptoms into major ones. While you may initially be sympathetic with the first few sick calls, after awhile it becomes a problem. A complicating factor can be that the person really is doing a good job when they are there, although their absence makes it hard to predict the work flow.

That's the problem Mary Beth faced when she worked as a supervisor at a government agency providing services for small businesses. One of her employees, Debbie, whose job was to do outreach to let businesses know about these services, was calling in sick about once a week for six months. Typically, Debbie would call in early in the morning and leave a message saying she couldn't make it because she didn't feel well, and then she would call in later in the day to say she still wasn't feeling well. After three months of this, she was no longer getting paid for the time off.

At first, Mary Beth was sympathetic, telling Debbie to take care of herself and get well. But then Mary Beth began to become suspicious. For example, when Debbie coughed, it sounded like she was just pretending to cough to show how sick she was. And then some-times when she left early, saying she wasn't feeling so well, Mary Beth wondered if this was really the case. Mary Beth suspected that maybe Debbie just had trouble dealing with the regular hours of the job. She had previously worked as circus barker, with no regular hours, as she traveled with the circus and recruited people on the streets to come to the circus. Mary Beth thought Debbie could well be making up excuses for not coming in because she was bored or had another more interesting event to attend.

Mary Beth felt that the obvious response was to talk to Debbie to express her concerns about the absences and check out her suspi-cions that Debbie was really sick. However, she hesitated taking any action because the other employees in the office, including several supervisors who managed employees doing administrative work, liked Debbie. She was very outgoing and affable, and they were espe-cially intrigued by the stories Debbie told of her experiences as a circus barker.

Then, too, Mary Beth felt uncomfortable about confronting Deb-bie, feeling that if cornered, Debbie could easily lie that she was really sick when she wasn't. In addition, the government agency had no policy about dealing with the situation of an employee who claimed to be sick when he or she wasn't. And when Debbie did come to work, she was very effective in her job doing outreach be-cause of her outgoing, bubbly personality. Of course, if she wasn't out on sick leave so much she could do so much more.

What Should Mary Beth Do?

In Mary Beth's place, what would you do and why? What do you think the outcomes of these different options would be? Here are some possibilities:

➲   Bite the bullet and confront Debbie about your suspicions to find out whether she really is sick or malingering.

➲   Don't worry about not having an official policy: if someone is taking a sick leave and lying about it—even if they aren't paid for that time—that's grounds for dismissal.

⮱ Don't rock the boat because Debbie has been doing a good job when she comes to work and the other employees like her.

⮱ Have a meeting with Debbie in which you explain that it's all right if Debbie wants to work shorter hours, but you just want her to be straightforward and not make excuses if she isn't really sick.

⮱ Don't try to find out why Debbie is calling in sick so much. Just tell her that even if she is doing a good job, she can't have so much sick leave time—and you will have to terminate if the excessive sick leave continues.

⮱ Other?

While excessive sick leave and making phony excuses may be a grounds for termination in many or most cases, in this case, Debbie has been doing a good job and is well-liked by other employees. It also seems like that the work is such that she doesn't need to be there as many hours as required for a full-time job.

Thus, it might be best to get everything out in the open with a frank conversation with Debbie in which you show you want to be understanding and sympathetic. Perhaps you might tell her up front that you have had some suspicions about her taking so many sick days in the past, but you just want her to be straight with you now and you'd like to work out an accommodation with her. If she wants to work four days a week rather than five, that would be fine. You just want her to tell you now what she'd like to do because you only want her to call in when she is really sick.

While not rocking the boat might continue the status quo of Debbie working four days a week by calling in sick to get the extra day, it is not a good idea to continue a working arrangement where you have suspicions and one of your employees is able to do what they want by lying. Such a situation, if not stopped, could lead the employee to come up with other lies. Also, it can leave you feeling manipulated and resentful, and that can lead to tension with this employee. Better to get your concerns out in the open and work out what is best for the organization after that. In this case that would seem to be Debbie working a shorter work week, and being honest about working these shorter hours rather than calling in sick to get this time off. This is the arrangement that Mary Beth reached with Debbie after having a candid face-to-face discussion of the situation.

Today's Take-Aways

☑ If an employee is calling in sick a lot, it could be they are sick—or may they just want the time off for other reasons.

☑ While taking excessive time off can be a good reason for firing an employee, sometimes it may be better for the organization if the employee does take off this extra time.

☑ Just as honesty is usually the best policy so is getting everything out in the open and clearing the air. If you suspect an employee is claiming to be sick, but really just wants more time off, getting at the truth is best medicine.

☑ While lying about sick leave is often grounds for firing an employee, if they aren't getting paid for their time off and are doing a good job, it may better to stand your ground to find out what's really going on and then do what's best for the company.

☑ There's a saying, "Act now and ask for forgiveness later." If the employee is otherwise doing a good job, it might be good to "forgive and move on" once you have everything out in the open and know the truth.

Scary Employee

Sometimes an employee may have major personal problems, but you may not be aware of them, either because the employee keeps those problems hidden or other employees don't tell you. This concealment is particularly likely when an employee is working with little supervision or has only occasional interaction with other employees so the personal problems don't surface and don't affect the operations of a team. Then, too, even if other employees are aware of the problems, they may not want to say anything. They may feel protective, don't want to be viewed as an informer, don't think it is their place to tell the boss about the problems of someone else, fear retaliation, or don't want to get involved for other reasons.

This is the situation which Gladys faced when she ran a small downtown hotel in a major city and hired Leonard, a man in his 30s, to take charge of the reception counter. He seemed to be the perfect employee—at least outwardly. He took on a lot of responsibility at the counter, from booking reservations, to collecting money, to telling the guests about where they might go while they were in the city. He also seemed to take great pride in his work; he came in every morning with lots of energy and enthusiasm, and big smiles for everyone. Since he seemed to take to responsibility like a duck to the water, Gladys gave him even more critical tasks to do, including keeping tax records and taking money to the bank.

Gladys felt secure that she could trust Leonard with just about everything and he seemed delighted to take on the additional assignments. She was especially relieved to be able to depend on him. She had only recently started running the hotel and she had already had to fire several other employees, mainly for being late or being unreliable, such as not showing up when they were supposed to work. Although she paid people well for the industry, many were working for only about $10 to $15 an hour in an industry with a high rate of turnover.

Then, after nearly a year, Gladys got some feedback from one of her regulars who stayed at the hotel whenever he came to the city on business trips that Leonard was acting very strangely and he had been almost afraid to register. As the guest described it, Leonard was extremely impatient while he looked through his wallet to find the card he wanted to use to register. Then Leonard stormed off, saying he would be back in awhile—"I've got some important things to take care of"—and he was gone for several minutes. Afterwards, the guest said he could feel Leonard glowering at him as he registered.

This information unnerved Gladys. However, when she spoke to other hotel employees, including the bellman and some of the cleaning staff, she learned Leonard had acted strangely with them and the guests sometimes. He would suddenly become very moody and irritable, and sometimes start yelling at them for no apparent reason. In a few cases, they even saw guests leaving without registering. So why hadn't they said anything before? "Because," Gladys explained, "I was under a lot of stress myself, having just taken over the hotel, and they didn't want to add to my stress. Also, the other employees saw that I was very dependent on Leonard, so they didn't feel the information would be welcome."

But now that she knew this information, Gladys wasn't sure what to do—and what should she do in the future to avoid having this kind of situation happen again.

What Should Gladys Do?

In Gladys' place, what would you do and why? What do you think the outcomes of these different options would be? Here are some possibilities:

➲ Fire Leonard immediately. He obviously seems to be nuts, which can't be good for business.

➲ Speak to Leonard and see if you can get him some medical or psychiatric help for his problem because he has been a good, reliable employee for so long.

➲ Recognize that Leonard probably has a bipolar or schizophrenic condition in which he can seem outwardly normal, but then will suddenly snap. Find a time to talk to him when he is acting normally. Then, tell him he has to get some help or you will fire him.

➲ Have a meeting or series of meetings with your current staff members to let them know you always will be receptive to hearing about problems in the hotel and really want to know about them in the future.

➲ Talk to Leonard about the report you have gotten about his behavior from a guest and a number of employees. See what led him to act as he did and then determine what you should do about the situation.

➲ Arrange to speak to Leonard, but have your lawyer there, because Leonard seems to be crazy and you're not sure what he will do.

➲ Other?

There are two problems here. One is convincing your other employees to feel comfortable confiding in you when they see a problem that you wouldn't normally be aware of. The other is what to do about Leonard now.

First, even though Leonard has been a long-time reliable employee, there apparently has been a long-standing problem, even though you have just found out about it. Then, too, Leonard is in a highly visible, responsible position where he is a front-line greeter for new and returning guests. Thus, it is a big risk to keep him on in such a position when you are not certain about his erratic behavior. Perhaps if he was in a behind-the-scenes desk job, you might take some time to try to help him overcome his problem. But he is in a critical front-line position, representing your hotel to your clients. So if there is a chance he may suddenly turn moody and scare guests away, this is a serious matter. Thus, it is best to let Leonard go. While you might explain why and give him a chance to explain, you already have heard about Leonard's behavior from numerous confirming sources, including a regular guest. Provide Leonard with whatever pay he is due, including any severance pay, and end the employment relationship now. Otherwise, with Leonard's behavior being so erratic, you can't be sure what he will do if you continue to keep him on the job.

In this situation, that is what Gladys ultimately did. She wavered for several days because she had become so dependent on Leonard and was worried about how quickly she could find someone else to do what she did. But finally, she recognized that she had become much too dependent on him, and had conveyed this to the other employees, making them afraid to tell her anything negative about him. "You can't let people hold you hostage," she observed. "No one is irreplaceable, and you have to make it clear to all your employees that no one has a special position in your company, such that they feel they are untouchable."

Then, to make such a situation less likely in the future, have a meeting with your employees, individually, in a series of small groups, or in a larger group, where you discuss what happened and ask your employees in the future to please inform you about any problems. Show them you are receptive and want to know about anything that can negatively affect your business, no matter how hard it may be to hear.

Today's Take-Aways

- ☑ While it can be very supportive to get someone who's mentally disturbed medical or psychiatric help, don't let their need for help jeopardize your business.

- ☑ If an employee is turning off your customers with his or her erratic behavior, it's time to turn that employee out.

- ☑ Just because an employee has been dependable and reliable for a long time doesn't mean they will continue to be. If necessary, be ready to change when they do.

- ☑ Just like machines, no employee should ever become indispensable. If things start to go haywire, you may need to find a replacement quickly for an essential task.

A Handful of Sex Problems

Sexual tensions can be a problem in the office, causing employees to be uncomfortable working together. This can be the case whether the problem involves suggestive comments, staring, groping, or an actual sexual relationship. Sometimes the problem starts with just innocent fooling around and teasing that escalates into an unwanted sexual advance or out-of-line comments. Other times it can come seemingly out of the blue, perhaps triggered by something alluring the other person is wearing. Whatever the reason, this is a problem that has to be nipped in the bud, so to speak, or it can poison the work environment and damage the business.

That's the problem Gregory confronted when he ran a trendy restaurant with about a dozen employees. He had several Hispanic employees who worked in the kitchen, including Raphael, the relative of several other employees—his son, a brother, and a cousin. They all spoke mostly Spanish, so they didn't mix much with the other employees. The non-kitchen staff included several waitresses and Lois, who worked at the counter taking orders and coordinating who gave what to which table. Lois also happened to have a large chest and often wore tight-fighting sweaters, which sometimes led to whispers and joking conversations about her assets by the male employees in the kitchen. Gregory wasn't aware of this, but he did know that Raphael "had the hots for Lois."

One day, as Lois went downstairs to the basement to get some supplies, Raphael suddenly reached out and grabbed her breasts and squeezed them. Immediately, Lois reacted with a hefty slap and rushed back upstairs, reporting what happened to Gregory, who had to decide how to deal with the incident. On the one hand, he felt such behavior shouldn't be tolerated. On the other, Raphael's actions seemed so out of the blue, and Raphael always had been a good worker. Plus, Raphael was at the center of a family network of kitchen employees, and he was concerned about how dealing with Raphael might affect the other employees.

What Should Gregory Do?

In Gregory's place, what would you do and why? What do you think the outcomes of these different options would be? Here are some possibilities:

➲ Fire Raphael immediately, and explain that such behavior simply won't be tolerated. Don't worry about his family members leaving; you can always find other employees if they do.

➲ Talk to Raphael and explain why what he did was wrong, recognizing that such behavior might be acceptable in Hispanic culture and that Raphael's relatives might leave if you try to discipline or fire Ralph.

➲ Tell Lois that she shouldn't wear such provocative clothing in the future.

➲ Have a meeting with Raphael and Lois in which you tell Raphael his behavior was wrong and have him apologize to Lois.

➲ Have a meeting with Raphael and Lois at which you tell Raphael his behavior was wrong, although understandable in light of Lois's way of dressing, and you tell Lois to wear more conservative clothes to work in the future.

➲ Have a meeting with everyone in the restaurant to tell them what happened and tell them that such behavior is wrong, and if anyone does anything like this again they will be fired.

⊃ Talk to Lois and see what she would like you to do about it: fire Raphael or talk to him about why what he did was wrong.

⊃ Other?

Because this is an out-of-the-blue unexpected incident involving just Lois and Raphael, it is probably best to deal with Lois and Raphael alone. It might stir up the pot unnecessarily to introduce additional and extraneous ingredients into the mix.

So what to do? A good approach is what Gregory actually did in this situation. He spoke to Lois, and supported her by telling her he thought this behavior was completely reprehensible and unexpected. He did not try to blame Lois for what she was wearing—the "she asked for it" approach to sexual harassment—because clothes should not be an invitation to do more than look and admire, certainly not to touch.

After supporting Lois so she would feel better about what happened, Gregory asked her to help him decide what to do and gave her two options; he could fire Gregory for what he did, or he could talk to Gregory about what happened. He presented these choices as two true options so she didn't feel any pressure to choose. As Gregory explained, "She was upset and I thought I needed to respect her feelings. So I asked her what to do." The result was that Lois told Gregory to just talk to Raphael because she didn't want to see him fired.

Lois is a fairly tough, forceful person who can take care of herself, so after being upset for a short time, she put the incident aside and didn't let her bother her anymore. Raphael has never bothered her again. While there might be a slight tension when they pass by each other, they work in separate sections of the restaurant and have little contact normally, so everything was soon back to normal as though the incident had never happened.

The advantage of this approach is that it combined talking to both Lois and Raphael. Gregory first supported Lois's hurt feelings and anger and helped her get over them, and he then talked to Raphael, telling him why what he did was wrong and admonishing him not to do what he did again. In this way, he dealt with both employees appropriately. While he didn't condone Raphael's actions, firing him on the spot might have been an overreaction because Lois, the aggrieved party, didn't want to see him fired. And telling Lois to avoid provocative clothing in the future would be out of line for an employee working in a behind-the-scenes job in an informal setting as well as suggesting that you blamed her for Raphael's actions. Additionally, since the two were already feeling tension towards each other, it was best not to immediately bring them together in a meeting about the incident where tempers could have flared up.

Today's Take-Aways

☑ If there's a single incident of sexual harassment, try resolving it first between the parties involved rather than bringing it out in the open and escalating it to involve the whole workplace.

☑ Treat any complaint of sexual harassment seriously—but remember it's just a report and there are two sides to every story.

☑ Make it clear that you think any sexual harassment is wrong, then give each side a chance to express their feelings about what happened to help you decide what to do.

Part IV

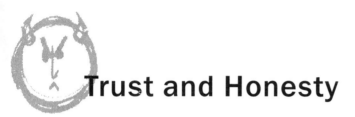

Trust and Honesty

Liar, Liar!

Lying has always been taken seriously in the workplace, but perhaps more so today in light of top executives, politicians, journalists, scientists, and others caught in lies. Prospective business students who exaggerated or included false information on their resumes were rejected from one prestigious university a few years ago. Several politicians have shamefully fessed up before resigning from office after their lies were exposed. Top executives, too, have been forced to leave their posts when their false credentials came to light. And then there were the book memoir scandals when authors were revealed for writing false or exaggerated accounts. Still, the payoff is so great for the liar who isn't caught that lying by employees and prospective employees remains a serious problem. And some liars are so good it's hard to catch them in the beginning, until that big lie is revealed, leaving employers and coworkers feeling like fools. But is there something you can do?

That's the problem that Eva, a human resources specialist, faced when she managed a division of professional employees for a recruitment agency. When she first hired James to be a recruiter, working on a draw against commission basis, he seemed the perfect candidate. He was in his late 20s, had movie star looks, and was very charming. People just loved to be around him, and he told great, amusing stories that had everyone enthralled during breaks.

Although he was new to the recruitment game, he seemed to learn quickly. Eva set him up in an adjacent office to hers. She told him what to do when he interviewed prospective employees and when he filed the necessary paperwork for placements with clients and job orders from clients. As a new hire, James wasn't expected to close a great many deals, but he soon was filing reports for the interviews he conducted and job orders he obtained. He even posted a few future placements for which he would earn a nice commission check after his initial draw was deducted. Meanwhile, he continued to charm Eva and others with his stories about his unusual experiences, such as his travels to exotic destinations like an archaeological trip down the Amazon and a mountain climbing trip to Tibet. No one suspected anything wasn't true because he was seemed so sincere and charming.

That's why Eva pushed aside the first off-the-job warning signs when she learned from a recruitment manager in another division, Ed, that James was dating a woman he knew. Eva thought it was odd that he was dating the woman because he was 20 years younger than the woman, who was in her late 40s and was overweight and unattractive. Ed told her that the woman, a successful professional, was lending James money and buying him clothes. While Eva thought James was playing this woman, she felt it wasn't relevant to his work for her. According to Eva: "How do you make judgments of someone's business integrity based on what he's doing off the job? I didn't think it right to do so, so I didn't let that knowledge—which I got simply because this other manager knew the woman he was dating—influence how I judged James as an employee."

But then came other warning signs, such as when James began missing work or coming in late although he always had a good excuse. His car broke down; he had to take a good friend to the hospital; his grandmother died; and so on. In turn, Eva and others in the office tried to be sympathetic and consoling, not thinking to doubt his claims.

Then, after he had worked for three months, James didn't come in for three days. Eva couldn't find him, even though she looked everywhere, calling his house, his girlfriend, the local hospitals, and the police. And then James called, claiming that he had been in the Marine Reserves and his unit was unexpectedly called on to go to Baghdad for a special mission so he was calling from there. But a day later the truth came out when James called Susan, the older woman he had been dating, to ask her to get him out of jail and she told her manager friend who in turn told Eva. Apparently, James had been cheating on Susan by dating another woman, and after he borrowed the woman's car and didn't return it, she called the police who arrested him, and now he was in jail in a nearby state, charged not only with stealing the car, but also with possessing drugs.

Eva immediately terminated him. Then, as she checked on the records James had previously filed for job orders, interviews, and placements, it turned out none of that was true. Rather, James had simply filed reports for placements, interviews, and job orders that didn't happen. Why? "Probably just to show activity," Eva surmised, "because he was already getting a draw and any commission wouldn't be paid until the person placed actually went to work." After that, further input from his cheated-on girlfriend and mother revealed that he had a long-time pattern of lying about everything. Even his mother had given up on him as a pathological liar. a problem compounded by his heavy use of drugs.

Certainly Eva was justified in firing James, who was still in jail in another state indefinitely at this point, and she never heard from him again. But is there anything she might have done early on that might have avoided the problem?

What Might Eva Have Done Differently?

Eva and others who worked with James were "completely fooled," as Eva put it, because James seemed so outwardly charming, engaging, and enthusiastic about the job. But was there anything that Eva might have done differently to keep from being taken in? In Eva's place, what would you do and why? What do you think the outcomes of these different options would be? Here are some possibilities:

⮞ Supervise James more closely in his first weeks on the job to see that he is doing the interviews, job orders, and placements effectively.

⮞ Randomly call a few clients to double-check that he has made the placements and to make sure the clients are happy with these placements.

➲ Be more suspicious about James's activities on the job once you learn about his deceptive behavior with a woman friend of another manager. Even if it's behavior off the job, it provides some insights into James character.

➲ Ask James for more details when he tells an amusing story that sounds especially amazing and notice if he is comfortable providing those details.

➲ Give James a second chance after he gets out of jail, if he assures you he will tell the truth in the future.

➲ Other?

Unfortunately, many pathological liars are oh-so-charming, and it is easy to be taken in by them. In fact, they may be so good at lying that even if Eva had asked James to supply more details for his stories, he could have easily come up with an expanded story and might have even enjoyed the challenge of showing off his cleverness. Then, too, being a cad off the job might not be evidence that someone is going to be deceptive in the workplace, because many people do separate how they act on the job from their personal life. While they may feel that "all's fair in love and war," as they say, they put on their professional hat in the workplace. Still, Eva might have trusted her feelings of suspicion once she learned that James was probably conning the other woman, given the discrepancy between his charm and much younger years—making him a highly desirable bachelor on the single's scene—and his gigolo-like relationship with an older, unattractive woman. Even if Eva was privy to this information through an unusual connection, once she knew this, she could certainly pay attention to this as a warning sign.

Additionally, Eva might have done more in James's first weeks on the job. Eva didn't do any checking, because it is not the normal practice in the recruitment industry to contact clients to ask how things are going with a recruiter. As Eva explained: "Many recruiters would quit over someone checking up on them like this. Most of them see themselves as independent professionals, and they would be insulted if a manager inserted himself into their relationship with the client. They see these people as their clients. In fact, if they move to another agency, they might take their clients with them."

However, in this case, James was new to the recruitment field, so Eva would be justified in checking on him more as part of his introductory training. One way might be to ask him to keep his door open in the first few weeks so she could easily come in to give him additional information and leads. Then she might be able to better hear and observe what he was doing, either from her office or when she walked by.

Additionally, she might have paid more attention when he began making excuses for not coming in or coming in late. Perhaps she could have accepted the first few without much question. But once the excuses became more frequent, she might have questioned him more closely or instituted a policy of taking some corrective action—such as docking his draw—for excessive absences.

In short, she might have been less trusting and more proactive in supervising and monitoring James's work in the beginning so he would be less likely to get away with his lies. Sure, it's great to trust employees and permit those who are good workers to take the initiative, to be more of a facilitative boss than a hands-on supervisor. But when an employee is new and still being tested, it can help to do more supervising and monitoring—not only to make sure the employee is off to a good start and knows how to do the job, but also to catch the occasional liar, who is usually facile and charming. That's why he or she can commonly get away with those lies.

Today's Take-Aways

- ☑ If your intuition or gut tells you that there is cause for concern, trust the feeling and check out what the person is doing and saying a little more.

- ☑ Don't let someone's outer charm fool you; the snake in the grass usually has a soft, smooth skin and moves stealthily until ready to strike.

- ☑ If someone is a deceptive liar off the job, he or she could be using the same tactics on the job.

- ☑ Don't just train someone in how to do the job. Check in on them afterwards for the first few days or weeks to be sure they are actually doing it and doing it well. If not, correct and advise them on what to do.

- ☑ If someone knows how to spin a good story, it may be that they know how to spin the truth, too.

It's the Little Things

Sometimes an employee can start off fine, then gradually do more and more to take advantages of gaps in the system or your own good nature. If they get away with one thing, they do a little more the next time. If confronted, they have a reasonable explanation and promise not to do it again. But then, time passes, and they do it again. Often what they do seems so small that you may not want to say anything to rock the boat—especially if they are doing a good job—afraid to interfere with employee productivity and morale. But left unchecked, the occasional times when the employee takes advantage can increase and can spread to other employees who start to take advantage as well.

It is like the *Field of Dreams* motto: "If you build it, they will come." Well, leave an opening in the system or your supervision, and employees will take advantage. As one of the employers I interviewed put it: "Employees are like little children who have to be supervised. They're continually testing you, checking on the limits. So if you don't have the checks in place, some will find gaps in the system and see what they can get away with. If they have an opportunity to take advantage and get some extras for themselves, they'll take that opportunity. So you've got to keep watching them and stop them when they start to do wrong."

That's the situation Dorothy faced when she opened up a small boutique and bookstore, which featured a mix of eclectic merchandise, from clothes and jewelry, to novelty gifts, books, and CDs. Since she also worked as a part-time community college instructor, she staffed her store with employees she felt could work on their own with minimal supervision: three women ranging in age from the late 20s to early 60s, who had all had some retail experience and professed a love of books. She was especially impressed with Beverly, the oldest of the group, who looked like everyone's favorite grandmother. She was always smiling and had such a reassuring manner that she made a great salesperson. Customers often asked for advice, and her soothing, helpful manner persuaded them to buy or buy more. So Dorothy thought of Beverly as her gem. "She was so sweet and innocent," Dorothy said. She trusted Beverly implicitly, and left her credit card with her for making last-minute purchases needed for the store, such as paying for a delivery or picking up supplies.

But then, after a few months, the little incidents started, although Dorothy didn't know about them at first. A few times, Beverly "borrowed" a book from the store and didn't return it. Dorothy didn't learn about this until she began some inventory checks three months later, wondered about the discrepancy between the books ordered, sold, and in inventory (called "shrinkage" by those in the business), and happened to see one of those books in Beverly's briefcase. When she was confronted, Beverly was mortified and stuttered that she had just "borrowed" the book and planned to return it. Dorothy told her not to do this because they were selling new books. She said it might be possible to get an extra sample from the vendor or Beverly could have it at a steep 30 percent employee discount. Then, thinking the problem resolved, Dorothy praised Beverly for her good work, hoping to end the discussion on a positive note.

Soon there were other incidents. One time Beverly used Dorothy's credit card for the store to get a haircut and buy some groceries, about $100 altogether. "Oh, I must have mixed up the credit card with my own," Beverly explained, and Dorothy simply deducted the amount from Beverly's next paycheck. Only later did it occur to Dorothy that Beverly might have also used her time on the job to get this haircut and buy the groceries at stores just down the block. But feeling the incident closed, Dorothy didn't ask.

A month later, though, Dorothy found another such charge on her card, and again Beverly apologized, even more profusely this time, promising it wouldn't happen again and she would be more careful. Once again, she quickly made restitution for the purchases she charged. And the time it took to make these purchases? "Oh, it was during my lunch break," Beverly assured her. From Beverly's hesitant, wavering voice as she answered, Dorothy felt maybe Beverly had really taken off during her work time, but felt there was no way to check to tell for sure.

Then, when Dorothy did another quarterly inventory and sales check, she discovered a number of discrepancies, not only for books but for some of the small novelties the store carried. Could it be Beverly taking things again or was this just ordinary shrinkage? Dorothy wasn't sure what to do.

What Should Dorothy Do?

The dilemma for Dorothy was not being certain if Beverly was helping herself to extras, not being sure how to best find out, and not knowing what to do about it if it turned out to be true. Outwardly, Beverly seemed like such a kind, trustworthy person, and she had been doing well in making sales. So what should Dorothy do? If you were in Dorothy's place, what would you do and why? What do you think the outcomes of these different options would be? Here are some possibilities:

⊃ Hire a private eye to do some checking to see if Beverly is properly ringing up sales at the cash register.

⊃ Ask another employee to keep an eye on Beverly when you are out of the store.

⊃ Call the police and say you suspect employee theft.

⊃ Have a frank discussion with Beverly about what you suspect and promise her no retribution if she admits what she has done.

⊃ Talk to Beverly about what you suspect and pay attention to her response. Even if she doesn't admit taking anything, terminate her employment if you still suspect she did it.

⊃ Skip having any discussions with Beverly because she probably won't admit anything and it's hard to tell if she did it otherwise. Instead, just fire her since you no longer trust her.

➲ Leave some new books and novelty items lying around in the backroom as bait and see if Beverly takes them.

➲ Other?

In this case, the amount in question is very small—only a few hundred dollars in books and small novelty items that Beverly may have taken, plus the two small credit card purchases, which may or may not have been intentional deceptions. Thus, whatever is missing doesn't amount to a serious crime. The police may think this is an internal civil matter anyway, so there's no need to call them except for having a record for insurance purposes. The police will at most ask you to file a report and then put it in the database. Bringing in a private investigator equally seems like overkill, given the small amount of inventory missing, and any inappropriate credit card charges are easily discovered once the statement arrives.

Certainly, you might mention something to all the employees about the discrepancies you have noticed, to put everyone on notice that you have a problem and discourage any further pilfering from your inventory. But it's best not to point the finger at Beverly to other employees because at this point, all you have are your suspicions and Beverly's claims of a mistake in the case of the two credit charges.

This leaves having a discussion with Beverly and deciding whether to give her the benefit of the doubt or let her go. In the case of stealing—even if it's the small stuff—it's generally best to terminate an employee. Once trust is gone, it's hard to get that back. If you're not able to supervise employees closely, you need to feel fully confident in those you permit to work on their own. Otherwise, an employee who has stolen once from you might simply work on doing it better the next time rather than shaping up and flying right. You just don't know, and it's a hard risk to take, particularly when you have a small operation and just a few employees.

So use the discussion to decide what to do about Beverly. Try to keep the conversation from becoming confrontational and create a more supportive environment for Beverly to confess what she did. You might start by telling Beverly about how much you have valued her as an employee and compliment the good work that she has done. Then, go over the various problems, noting the two charges on your credit card, the work time used to make these purchases, the book you saw Beverly taking home in her briefcase, and the discrep-

ancies in the inventory. See how she responds, noticing her body
language as well as what she says. Does she admit what she has
done, thinking you will be supportive, and does she seem remorse-
ful? Does she admit some but not all, and raise your suspicions by
appearing nervous and evasive? Does she deny everything except the
book which you actually saw—and do you believe her? It will probably be a tense, uncomfortable conversation for both of you, but it
should help you decide what to do.

If she admits the thefts or is evasive and you still suspect her,
it's best to let her go because you don't know if you can trust her
again. You can always use the wrongful credit card charges as
grounds for termination because that could actually be a crime.
That's exactly what Dorothy did do in this case, after Beverly admit-
ted to borrowing a few books but not to taking any of the missing
novelty items. She told Beverly that even if she had only taken a few
books and none of these items, she had still used her credit card
incorrectly, and she couldn't have an employee working for her who
could make such a mistake. She needed someone with more attention to detail. Dorothy felt she could no longer trust Beverly, even if
she had been a good employee. She used the credit card mistakes as
a diplomatic way of saying goodbye rather than saying that she still
suspected Beverly of a series of small, though probably unprovable,
thefts.

Alternatively, you may feel confident that Dorothy was only involved in making the credit card mistakes and taking a few of the
books before you confronted her about this. Then you might give her
the benefit of the doubt that the problem stopped when you spoke
to her and the later discrepancies were due to other factors. But continue to monitor what she is doing as best you can in the future,
perhaps by asking the other employees to be more attentive in looking for anyone taking any merchandise (without mentioning Beverly
by name). Then if you suspect Beverly in the future, it's time to let
her go.

Today's Take-Aways

☑ The little things can not only mean a lot; they can cost a lot if
you let them go.

☑ Just like oaks grow from little acorns, little acts of theft and deception can keep growing, so stop them while they are still little.

☑ While any employee can make an honest mistake, if it happens again, it may not be so honest.

☑ The beginnings of employee deception and theft often start when you are not paying attention. Leave the door of opportunity wide open to steal from you, and employees may walk through.

☑ Don't take chances with distrust growing; consider it like a mold on your business. Once it takes root, get rid of it by getting rid of the employee you distrust.

Over a Barrel

What happens when an employee who has been given increased responsibility uses the new position of power to demand even more? What if that employee thinks this position can be used as a negotiation ploy to seek increased compensation because of feeling that he or she has been underpaid or undervalued? Are such tactics fair, or are they taking advantage of the situation? While some employees may see tactics as part of the game to get ahead, employers may be much less receptive, feeling they are placed in a squeeze by an unscrupulous employee. They feel such tactics are akin to extortion or blackmail; they feel that they are being put "over a barrel."

That's the situation Chad, the owner of a game and toy manufacturing company, faced when he hired Pierre, an employee in Canada, to handle marketing and sales to help the company expand there. Initially, Pierre's job was just to set up game fairs and conventions in Canada, and handle product sales of board and card games at those events. Chad paid him a salary, plus a percentage of game sales. While Chad paid the salary directly, Pierre deducted his percentage from the sales and sent Chad the balance.

The first six months went well. Then, when Chad had some problems with a distributor for eastern Canada, he asked Pierre if he wanted to set up distribution for the company as a sales rep. Besides giving Pierre a larger salary, he added performance bonuses, plus the percentage of game sales at the events. Pierre offered to store some of the product inventory in his house and Chad said fine. Although Pierre mentioned that he had gotten about twice as much in salary when he did similar work setting up distribution for another company several years before, Chad pointed out that those kind of salaries were a thing of the past in the industry. They had been inflated by the dot.com boom, but now those times were over and the salary Chad was offering was in line with the industry standard, maybe even a little higher. So Pierre agreed.

Over the next few months, Pierre set up arrangements with a network of retailers and Chad's company shipped product, generally to Pierre, who then broke up the shipments to send on to retailers and collected payments from them. He was supposed to send a report to Chad for all of these sales, along with all the funds he collected, less his salary. At the same time, he worked on setting up the big annual game fair.

As agreed, he sent the first two reports along with the funds he collected, about $20,000 in receipts minus his salary. But then, over the next three months, he sent nothing. When Chad asked about the delay, Pierre said he was working on the reports. He explained that, "You don't understand how hard it is to set up these accounts" and noted that he now had an entire room devoted to keeping the inventory. But if he was dissatisfied with the agreed-upon salary, performance bonuses, or commission on sales at the event, he didn't mention this. Nor did he ask for any compensation for keeping the inventory in his house.

Still, concerned about the lack of reports, Chad hired an outside industry consultant to look into the situation and give him some feedback on what Pierre was doing. Was Pierre just incompetent or not to be trusted? After a month, the consultant, who conducted some interviews with Pierre, reported back to Chad that he just felt Pierre was disorganized and ashamed to admit he couldn't account for part of the returns and the money, but seemed like a honest guy. So Chad felt reassured and gave Pierre an extension, but said it was very important for him to know how the company was doing in sales in Canada. He even flew Pierre to company headquarters to go over how things were going, review how to do the reports, and discuss the company's plans for the future. "I'll get right to it," Pierre assured him, although it took him a month to finally send a report for three previous months, along with about $15,000. When Chad reviewed the reports, he had some questions since there were discrepancies between the summary and the activity breakdowns for the several months of sales in the report.

Then, a week before the big game convention, Chad received an e-mail from Pierre in which Pierre stated all the ways in which he was dissatisfied and felt his compensation was unfair. He said that part of their agreement was that he would use his own company to import the company's products, but he wasn't being compensated for that. He also felt he should be getting some compensation for the inventory he stored in his house and suggested about $500 a month—a figure Chad thought was far more than it would cost to put the inventory in another facility or storage locker. And then he asked for a 12.5 percent commission on the retail product sales in addition to the salary he was already getting, when, according to Chad, even the best reps working on a commission get 5 percent. He concluded by stating that unless he could work on such a "fair" agreement with Chad for his work, he wouldn't import any products for the upcoming convention.

Chad was furious because he felt Pierre was taking advantage of the upcoming event to gouge him for more money. And because Pierre was collecting the money for sales, he could use that as leverage as well. Chad explained: "I called Pierre and told him 'No,' because I don't have the most recent reports, so I don't know if we are making money and I don't even know what's in the bank account. He told me, 'Then I won't sell any products at the event.' Well, that's an important event and now he takes this critical time to ask for more money or else. It's extortion, but he's holding all the cards right now because of this big event that's coming up." Chad was still deciding what to do with only a day or two left to make a decision.

What Should Chad Do and What Might Chad Have Done Differently?

In Chad's place, what would you do and why? What do you think the outcomes of these different options would be? And what do you think Chad might have done differently? Here are some possibilities for what to do now:

➲ Tell Pierre what he is doing is extortion, and if he refuses to acknowledge your original agreement, you will contact the police in Canada.

➲ Call the police in Canada, tell them you are being blackmailed, and ask them what to do. They can monitor any agreement you make under duress and then possibly arrest Pierre after the big event.

➲ Agree to the terms Pierre has asked for, since he has the money from which he will deduct any salary, commissions, and rent for the inventory. But afterwards, fire him and hire someone else to do what he was doing, or set up your own office in Canada.

➲ Recognize that the additional funds Pierre is asking for are fair, although his timing is wrong in asking for them just before the convention.

➲ Consider Pierre's request for more compensation just before the big event to be a negotiating ploy by him and seek to negotiate a compromise deal.

➲ Postpone or cancel the event and tell Pierre you won't agree to a change in terms. Demand that he send you an accurate report along with the money due to you, and if he doesn't, you will sue him.

➲ Other?

A big problem is that Chad gave Pierre too much control of handling operations in Canada, including control of the money, before he had fully determined that Pierre could handle this successfully. Yes, Pierre had proved effective in a more limited way, putting on some events and handling sales there, although the product was actually shipped in by a distributor. While Pierre had had some experience setting up distribution for another company, Chad didn't checked into how well he had performed for this other company. In fact, he couldn't, since this company was no longer in business, a victim of the dot.com bust. Also, it made sense to think of Pierre when Chad decided to find another source of distribution because his first distributor was doing a bad job. However, he might have waited until he was sure about how well this new arrangement might work before cutting off his agreement with his first distributor entirely—a realization that Chad recognized in hindsight. Instead, he placed too much trust in Pierre too soon.

In addition, Chad didn't notice the red flags that popped up when Pierre noted that he had previously made twice as much with another company. Although Chad countered by pointing out that the industry had changed so the payments were less now, this still could have been a sore point causing resentment for Pierre. Chad might have paid more attention to how things were playing out. For example, by not sending timely reports and holding onto the money longer than he should, Pierre might have been delaying because he felt he should be taking out more. Whatever the reason, if Chad wasn't getting the reports and money after the first two months of their arrangement, he should have held off shipping any more product until he got them. Then, if Pierre still didn't send them after a few weeks, he might have hired someone else.

But what to do now? First, while Pierre's actions may amount to extortion, any threat to report Pierre to the police for his threat amounts to extortion, too. So you should definitely not threaten to report him to the police in retaliation. The police strategy may not work well anyway because you and Pierre have already had a relationship for almost a year, and the police could easily regard Pierre's threat to withhold delivering product to the game event as a civil matter based on a contract and payment dispute. So forget involving the police or threatening police involvement.

Instead, divide what to do into two stages: what to do about the event itself, and what to do afterwards. Because this is a very important annual event where you depend on good sales for your company, it would be best to not try to postpone or cancel the event. Certainly, had Pierre contacted you a month or two before with his request for more compensation, this might have made for a more reasonable, fairer proposal to discuss and renegotiate an agreement which Pierre felt was unfair. You could have discussed this and perhaps increased the package, avoiding this last-minute standoff. But since he waited until just before the big event, the request for more compensation is not a fair negotiating ploy; it is really a form of blackmail, although you can do little about it under the pressure of the conference.

Chad actually decided to agree to Pierre's terms rather than trying to negotiate a deal on the brink, which could have undermined the show. Pierre had to make the shipping arrangements immediately, so there was really no time to negotiate anything. Obviously that's why Pierre had sent this all-or-nothing ultimatum. So go ahead, agree, and let the event go forward based on agreeing to all Pierre's demands. Let him assume that your relationship will continue after the event, insisting that he needs to now send you a timely report, along with the money after he has deducted his salary, commissions, and rent for the inventory.

But afterwards, once you have gotten the report and the money, fire Pierre—which is what Chad did. Chad hired the consultant he had used to report on Pierre to take over what he was doing. If you want even tighter control in the future, consider setting up your own office or franchise in Canada rather than hiring another employee.

In short, put aside your feelings of outrage over Pierre's demands at first. Instead, do what's pragmatic, which is to go on with the show by meeting Pierre's demands. Arrange to get what money you can from Pierre by letting him think you expect to continue the arrangement. But then once you have your money, so Pierre has no more hold over you, let him go, and then carefully decide on what to do to have someone else do what Pierre was doing in the future.

Today's Take-Aways

☑ If an employee tries to use extortion or blackmail to get something from you, don't fall into the trap of trying to extort him yourself by threatening to go to the police.

☑ Don't let your outrage over an employee's actions, no matter how unethical or wrong, blind you to doing what's strategic and practical. While acting on your anger will help you feel better at the time, being pragmatic will help you do better—and ultimately feel better, too.

☑ Sometimes a two-stage approach can work best if you are forced to take some action now: Do what you have to do to stay afloat now, then set your course so you can sail ahead faster in the future.

☑ If necessary, take on some extra ballast now, but then in the future, look for the first opportunity to get rid of it.

Con Job

Would you be able to tell if a prospective employee was a con artist before hiring him or her or after a few weeks on the job? Sometimes it is very hard to tell because the con artist is the master of charm and smooth talking. He or she looks the part and talks the talk. And when the con seems to be up, he or she walks away. There may be a trail of conned employers left behind. But in this age of being afraid to say anything bad about a former employee for fear of being sued, you may not be able to find out anything. Or the companies the person previously worked for may be out of business—in fact, the con's con may have helped in that regard. So how do you know and what do you do?

That's the situation Fred, a sales manager for a computer equipment company in the L.A. area, encountered when he hired Hugh as an outside salesman. Hugh had a great resume, indicating several years of sales for other computer manufacturing companies. Since these companies were now out of business, they couldn't be contacted for references. Hugh was a very personable, smooth talker—seemingly the perfect man for the job. Duly impressed, Fred hired him for a job that offered a draw against commission arrangement, plus expenses such as gas and phone calls. He waived the usual background check because Hugh's previous jobs had been for now-defunct businesses, which Hugh attributed to the dot.com bust and a continuing shakeout and takeover in the field. Also, Hugh had such an aura of success, it seemed hard to doubt him. He drove a fancy new car, dressed in expensive designer suits, and used a picture cell phone with all the latest gadgets. He came off, as Fred observed, "like a guy used to making a lot of money."

Fred gave Hugh a list of local firms to contact, and over the next few weeks, Hugh seemed to be doing a great job. He would come into the office, make a few phone calls—presumably to leads—and then leave the office for the day, presumably to call on these new accounts. However, after a few weeks, Fred began to be suspicious of what Hugh was doing. When he ran into some executives from some of the companies Hugh said he had been contacting at a business mixer, they said, no, Hugh hadn't contacted them. Hugh had a ready excuse: He had spoken to other people at the company and was still working out the details of the order. When Fred got his first expense accounting from Hugh, there was a larger number of miles and a higher amount for meal reimbursements than Fred expected. But Hugh explained that, too—in his enthusiasm for the job, he simply saw more clients and spent more on lunches with these clients.

Then, for a few weeks, Hugh was frequently away from work for various reasons. Following an earthquake, he claimed his house was damaged so he couldn't go to work. Then, he had to deal with some flooding.

When Fred tried to pin Hugh down, he found him elusive. As Fred described it, "I could never find out where he was. He had no information about who he was calling on. One time, another salesman caught him saying he was in one place when he was in another. He explained he had to stop for something on the way."

Fred went with Hugh on some calls, and nothing seemed to go right. "I told him to set up some calls and I drove around with him. But the places we stopped, the guys had no interest. In another case, the guy we went to see had a single office, and we were selling networked systems of computers. And when we went on cold calls, he wasn't able to get in. So I felt something was definitely wrong."

As a result, Fred went to his own boss, the president of the company, and told him that Hugh simply wasn't producing and was a "lost cause." When HR confronted Hugh about Fred's complaints, he said he would resign and agreed to pay back the draw he had gotten for three months, but he never did. When Fred wrote to him to ask about this, the letters were returned as "undeliverable." Hugh had simply disappeared, and Fred speculated he had been a phony all along. "He just pulled the wool over everyone's eyes. He could have had another job. He could have been looking for another job. Who knows? He just got a good draw from us for the first three months, and that seems to be what he wanted."

The experience left Fred wondering how he could have been so completely fooled and what he could do differently in the future to avoid being taken in again.

What Could Fred Have Done Differently and What Should He Do in the Future?

Although Fred and others in the company were taken in, is there anything he might have done differently in the past to avoid being conned. In Fred's place, what would you do and why? What do you think the outcomes of these different options would be? Here are some possibilities for what to do:

- ➲ Be immediately suspicious if someone who is looking for a job is very well-dressed and has an expensive car.
- ➲ Be very suspicious if most or all of a person's references are companies that are out of business, making it impossible to check references there.
- ➲ Ask for other types of references if you can't do a check on previous employment in out-of-business companies, such as the names of previous employees, customers, or clients.
- ➲ If all or most of the references are out-of-business companies, probe more closely to find out why they failed.
- ➲ Accompany the new employee on outside sales calls to check on performance in the first few weeks; don't wait until you become suspicious.
- ➲ Make some random follow-up calls to people the new employee says he has contacted to see if he actually made these calls and how well he did on them.
- ➲ Other?

Certainly, it is hard to detect a con and you can easily be fooled because con artists are generally good at what they do. The real pros have perfected the art of the con, so they are slick, smooth, and have a ready answer when questioned about apparent gaps and glitches in what they say or do. They use appearances to deceive—just like the old saw says, appearances can be deceiving—and they take advantage of people's desire to believe and trust what seems to be true and good.

But there are ways to reduce your chances of being conned, as Fred pointed out himself, in thinking about what happened and considering what he would have done in hindsight.

First, you don't have to necessarily be suspicious if someone looking for a job is very well-dressed and has an expensive car. But don't take those as signs the person must have performed successfully in previous jobs. Rather, keep an open mind and treat the person's appearance as just one more factor to be considered. It can show the person was very successful and knows how to dress for success—or the person may be using appearances to deceive. You just don't know, so you should gather additional facts to fill out the picture.

Regard a list of previous references that can't be checked out as a possible warning sign. It's possible that the person just had a run of bad luck in getting hired by a string of companies that went out of business. But perhaps the person could be using such references to hide behind—or even worse, maybe he or she had something to do with the company's failure. So probe to learn more about what the person did and the reasons for the company's failure. And then look for alternate sources of references, such as other employees the person worked for or with at those companies. And if the person was dealing with customers and clients for the company, ask to use some of those as a reference and contact them.

If the person passes those initial hurdles, do more to check on performance right after the person is hired, even if the employee spends much of his or her time in the field. For example, Fred thought he might have accompanied Hugh on his sales calls in the first two or three weeks of his employment rather than waiting until he became suspicious later on. This way, you can not only provide the new employee with feedback and modeling on how to do a good job, but you can determine if the employee seems to be less experienced than he or she claimed when first hired.

Making some phone calls to check on whether your new em-

ployee is doing well can also help. Again, you should do this soon
after hiring the employee, not wait until you become suspicious.
With an outside employee, check over expense records early on and
question anything that looks overly expensive or unwarranted.

You may not be able to escape every con, but by checking early
and well, you may be able to detect early in the game that an employee is trying to con you and show that employee the door. If the
employee sees you are carefully checking, he or she may realize that
the con won't get very far and will soon leave, reducing any losses
that might result from the con.

Today's Take-Aways

☑ Like mushrooms, a con artist employee thrives in the darkness.
So shed some light on what the con is trying to do by checking
up on what he or she has done or is doing for you.

☑ To protect yourself against a con, use some con protection—a lot
of checking so you don't give the employee a chance to use a
blank check on you.

☑ Don't go by initial appearances or smooth confident words;
probe further to see what lies behind those appearances and
words.

☑ Use a two-step process in checking out new employees. Check if
what he or she says checks out before you hire; then check on
what he or she does in the first weeks after you hire.

26

Pay or Play

What do you do when an employee appears to be trying to scam you by using government regulations to take advantage of you and get extra money? The employee's actions are a little like the slip-and-fall con that is sometimes pulled in supermarkets or other big retail stores; the person suddenly falls as if there was something on the floor, and then they seek an insurance settlement. Well, some employees try to play the system in a similar way, and use legal action, complaints to regulatory agencies, or the threat of a lawsuit or complaint to force a settlement. Are there any protections you can institute to avoid being sucked into such a scam?

That's the situation JoAnn, an employee staffing manager, had to face when she worked at a temporary employment agency that placed people on a short-term basis. While the company where the employee was placed was in charge of directing and supervising that employee, the agency was the employer of record and in charge of paying the employee for the number of hours worked.

The problem developed when she placed Rich in a retail sales position in an electronics appliance store where he worked for two to three days for six weeks. As part of the placement, he was supposed to turn in time sheets each week, but he didn't turn them in on time. Each week, JoAnn had to make numerous calls to remind him to get in his time sheets, but she found him hard to reach. He wasn't at home; he didn't answer his cell phone; and if she called him at work and left a message, he was typically out or on the floor. When she left a message, he didn't call her back. She did manage to reach him a few times, but he told her he was busy and couldn't talk. He did return a couple of calls and he did turn in his payroll forms for the first two weeks.

After he left the job, JoAnn tried to call him numerous times because she still had several payments pending for him, awaiting his paperwork. JoAnn thought his lack of response was curious. He only had to turn in a few pages of information and then he would get paid. But after calling and leaving messages on his phone and cell phone, and sending him an e-mail reminder, she heard nothing. She figured the ball was in Rich's court, and when he realized he had to get in his paperwork in order to get paid, he would finally provide it.

Instead, several weeks later, soon after the 30-day payment period had expired, she got a notice from the Labor Board stating that Rich had complained he hadn't gotten paid and indicating a date for a hearing. JoAnn was amazed because she had tried so hard to get Rich paid, but he hadn't responded. And now he was complaining that her agency hadn't paid him. Why would he do that? She was suspicious at once. The Labor Board had a policy that an employee could win an award that basically matched the amount he hadn't been paid for up to 30 days. In other words, Rich could double the amount he had earned from the job.

Her suspicions weren't good enough to defeat Rich's claim. As a result of the hearing, the agency had to pay him a substantial settlement. There was no written record of JoAnn's many calls to get Rich paid, and the burden was on the agency to show what it had done. Needless to say, JoAnn's agency never heard from Rich again, and she certainly wouldn't have placed him again if they did. There was no evidence that Rich had actually created a scam to get more money by complaining to the Labor Board. But JoAnn was sure it was, and she wondered if this was a scam Rich was perpetrating on a number of companies.

What Should JoAnn Have Done and What Might She Do in the Future?

JoAnn never knew for certain if this was a scam. Assuming it was, what might she have done differently to prevent becoming a victim of an employee pay scam, and what might she do in the future to prevent this from happening? In JoAnn's place, what would you do and why? What do you think the outcomes of these different options would be? Here are some possibilities:

➲ Tell Rich that he has to bring in his paperwork if he wants to keep working for the agency. Give him a week's deadline; if he doesn't bring it in, cancel his work arrangement with the retail store.

➲ Do a more thorough background examination of his past work history and how long he was at previous jobs. If he had a series of short-term jobs, consider that a warning bell and check further into why they were so short.

➲ Contact his last few work references, not just the references he first provided. If he left amicably, that's a good sign. Otherwise, if the past employers will say little or nothing, consider that a warning to check further.

➲ Fully document all your efforts to contact him to be paid so you have a chronology showing exactly when you tried to reach him and what number you called. Then you can show how hard you tried and how persistent you were. If necessary, you can even obtain the phone records to show in court.

➲ Contact the police or district attorney's business practices unit to let them know you think you have been the victim of an employee payment scam and see what they advise.

➲ Other?

While more extensive background checks certainly might be a way to better avoid potential scams, they also may not be practical. This was, in fact, a problem at JoAnn's agency. They checked a few references and asked some questions about recent jobs, the length of employment, and reason for leaving, but it would take too long and cost too much to fully check out all references and employment claims. Instead, they had to depend on supplementing the limited background check with a gut-level feeling based on conducting numerous interviews of whether or not this employee was on the level. Occasionally, the bad apple would get through. It was just not cost-effective to do more, as is often the case when you have to hire many employees and fill the positions in a few days time.

It also may not be practical or productive to contact the police or district attorney. If you don't have some evidence to show there was a crime, they will do little more than take a report. Or they may be likely to treat this as a civil matter, such as a pay dispute. Without evidence of someone systematically using a payment scam on multiple employers, the police or the district attorney will generally feel they don't have enough to treat this as a crime.

However, you could establish some mandatory requirements to continue working for your placement service. If the necessary paperwork isn't filed by a certain date, there is no more work until the records are brought up to date. Such an ultimatum may be harder to enforce if a placement turns into a two-or-more-month job, because then the employee already has the position. But if you want to play hardball, you could tell Rich's supervisor on his latest job that Rich has to provide you with some paperwork or you will be replacing him with someone new. Then, if that still doesn't stir up the paperwork, take the action you promised—end Rich's employment and find a replacement.

Finally, do keep full documentation of all your attempts to pay Rich, including every phone call regardless of whether you reach him, leave a message or can't get through. This way you show both your good faith efforts Rich's lack of response and evasiveness, and you are in a better position in this case when you go to court. And this is something to do in the future as well to be better prepared should an employee try to scam you.

Today's Take-Aways

- ☑ You may not be able to avoid every employee scam, but keeping careful documents will help you defend against one.

- ☑ When you do background checks, pay particular attention to the length of time on previous jobs. If someone has had many jobs in a short time, consider that a warning sign that you've got a "hop-a-long" on your hands.

☑ When your intuition sets off warning bells, that's usually a good sign that you should check further because something doesn't feel right.

27 A Favor Backfires

Using your position to help out a friend can sometimes be a risky business, especially when you place great trust in a friend's referral and don't institute the usual checks. Certainly, connections through friends and other personal acquaintances are one of the major sources of employment—and generally getting good employees through networking works out. But when it doesn't, the results can be even worse because not only is the employee a problem, but the friendship can be threatened, too.

That was the situation that Frank, the owner of a small health club, faced when his good friend, Terrence, called to say he had a cousin who was recently downsized out of his administrative assistant position. He really needed something immediately, even part-time, so he wouldn't lose his apartment. "His cousin can't afford the security deposit on a new place," Frank explained. "And he would have a hard time moving back home with his parents."

Frank agreed to hire Terrance's cousin, Phil, for a few hours a day to write up and file reports. It was work that Phil could do with little supervision and he could choose his own hours, so Frank thought the arrangement ideal for someone who was between jobs. And he felt good being able to help out a friend.

When Phil arrived the first day, Frank set up a small office for him where he could work undisturbed, and he showed him how to clock in and out each day. Since Phil assured him he knew what he was doing, Frank left him alone while he worked with other employees who needed more supervision.

But after a few months, Frank realized there was a serious problem. He discovered it one day when he tried to call Phil to locate some files in his office for him, but Phil wasn't there. When he came to the office to get the files himself, he saw Phil having a leisurely lunch at a café down the street. And then, when Phil returned about 20 minutes later at the end of his shift to turn in his time sheet, Frank saw that he had included the hours he had been lunching at the café in his hours. When he asked Phil about it, Phil had a ready answer: "I was feeling lightheaded, so I felt I needed to eat something." So this time, Frank let the matter pass, figuring that this was a one-time occurrence.

This proved not to be the case. Over the next few weeks, as Frank learned from other employees who were aware of Phil's coming and goings, Phil was repeatedly taking off for the day and charging the company for the full three hours a day he agreed to work when, in fact, he actually worked only one or two hours. At first, Frank hesitated talking to Phil about the discrepancy because of their mutual friendship with Terrance. He hoped that things would work themselves out, because Phil appeared to be at least writing up and filing the reports he was supposed to be doing.

But finally things came to a head when Frank came into the office, heard Phil on the phone having a personal conversation with a friend, and found Phil's sweatshirt, jeans, sneakers, and underwear swirling around in the washing machine in the back of the office. At once, Frank went into Phil's office to speak to him, and instead of being apologetic for making personal calls and doing his laundry on company time, Phil became immediately huffy, exclaiming: "You're not respecting my privacy." He didn't even try to justify what he had been doing. Instead, he gathered up his things and angrily stormed out, saying: "I can't work here anymore. You're just too manipulative." Then, he slammed the door behind him. He did call a few days later to pick up his check for his hours worked so far. Frank paid him, not wanting to stir up the pot even more, particularly since Frank had been referred through a still good friend.

The experience left Frank feeling unnerved. He felt his good trust had been betrayed, especially since he had found a job for Phil to both respond to the request of a friend and to help Phil through a difficult period in his life But now he felt taken advantage of and misused and wasn't sure what to do next.

What Should Frank Do Now and What Might He Have Done Differently?

For Frank, one issue is what to do about Terrence, the friend who referred Phil; another is how to handle Frank's departure; and then there is the question of what to do about referrals from friends in the future. And was there anything Frank might have done differently to prevent the problems with Frank that occurred? In Frank's place, what would you do and why? What do you think the outcomes of these different options would be? Here are some possibilities:

- ⊃ Don't pay Phil the full amount he is claiming; explain you know he has been goofing off or looking for full-time work much of the time on the job, all the while charging you for the time worked.
- ⊃ Call Terrence to tell him how Phil took advantage of you, even if you risk losing the friendship.
- ⊃ Don't hire friends, or friends of friends, in the future; such employees might try to take advantage of your good nature and you could lose a good friend.
- ⊃ Consider the friend or friend of a friend just like you would any other employment candidate in deciding whether to hire that person in the first place. Don't provide a job just to help someone out.
- ⊃ Spend more time supervising a friend or a friend's friend, to be sure they are really doing a good job. Otherwise, you may be apt to trust the employee more because he or she has been referred by a friend.
- ⊃ Other?

While it might be tempting to want to help out a friend—and you may sometimes want a friend to help you out—it's also important to remind yourself that you are running and managing a business. You should have certain safeguards in place to make sure the person not only knows how to do the job, but is committed to do it well, just as you would in hiring any other employee. Let the person know that you have to do this and need to keep your feelings of friendship separate from your role as an employer. This way, you don't have to make a blanket policy of not hiring any friends or friends of friends at all. You just have to approach whether you do, for what positions, and under what circumstances, as a business decision.

Secondly, since you have paid Phil in the past, despite his using much work time for personal business, it is probably best to simply pay him now for the hours he is claiming. It can be messy to try to argue this after having set a precedent of previously paying him. Such a pay dispute could lead to a case against you in small claims court, hard feelings from your friend if he takes Phil's side, and a possible filing against you with the various regulatory agencies that oversee small businesses.

Finally, it's important to give your friend honest feedback about what happened, particularly since your friend might be getting the other side of the story from Phil. Your friend may not be aware of how severely Phil screwed up, and he should know so he is cautious about referring Phil again. But be careful to avoid casting blame on the friend. Give him the benefit of the doubt for not knowing about Phil's problems as an employee. Keep in mind that you had a choice as to whether to hire Phil and could have done more to check out his credentials before hiring him. Plus you might have taken steps to check out his performance while on the job rather than putting so much trust in him. So it's not the friend's fault and you shouldn't lay the blame on him.

In sum, be open to referrals from friends or even hiring friends in the future. But be sure to treat any hires like any ordinary business decision. It can be fine to hire a friend or friend's referral, all other things being equal. Just be sure they really are equal, and that you are equally careful to check up on how that person is working out early on. Don't let your relationship with the friend or the person making the referral blind you to doing due diligence when you make the hiring decision or check on how the person is performing once he or she is on the job.

Today's Take-Aways

☑ Friends and business may not always mix, but they can if you put the business first and let your friends know that this is what you have to do.

☑ Treat a friend or referral of a friend like any other employee, and let them know that you have to do this, too.

☑ Once you feel an employee is taking advantage of you, it's generally a good idea to talk to employee right away and try to work out a resolution. Don't let being friends with the employee or the employee's friend stand in your way.

On the Side

Moonlighting can create difficulties when employees don't know where to draw the line between what is acceptable off-the-job employment or business activity and what crosses the line. This has become an increasing problem because today, many employees have side businesses, such as selling health and beauty products or putting on sales parties once in awhile. And some employees have second jobs to pay the bills or for personal or career growth. Generally, this is fine as long as the employee isn't working for a competing business and keeps the outside employment or business off the job, except for the occasional—very occasional—phone call or copying, with permission required. But what if the employee increasingly pushes the edge? At what point does the employee go over the line of what's acceptable?

That's the situation Derek faced with Sally, who for three years had been doing PR and marketing for his small company that manufactured pet novelty products. Sally's job involved sending out press releases, contacting companies (like banks and pet shops) to set up premium promotions, running booths at trade and consumer shows, and organizing some promotional events to attract press attention to new products. In general, Derek was pleased with the work Sally was doing, and he found her outgoing, bubbly personality a good fit for the job.

On the side, Sally was selling nutritional supplements and putting on occasional sales parties for the products. There was no conflict with the company's pet line, and Derek was aware that Sally was selling the products. One day she mentioned the program to him and invited him to try some samples, which he declined. Sometimes she made phone calls to confirm after-work appointments. Initially, she had asked Derek for permission, which he had given, and then from time to time she made a few phone calls without asking. She also sold a few products to some of her coworkers. However, she was doing a good job for Derek's company, and the calls and sales he was aware of seemed to be only an occasional activity. So he didn't say anything to Sally, figuring she was using her good judgment to keep her part-time business off the job.

But then one day, Derek felt that Sally had gone too far. It happened at a party Derek put on to promote his company's latest line of treats and furniture for dogs and cats. He decided to turn it into a community-wide celebration, to which people were invited to bring their own pets and participate in a series of competitions. Meanwhile, Derek had several tables of products for sale. Sally and some other employees were responsible for handling product demonstrations and sales, as well as running the competitions and buying and setting out the snacks and drinks for the party. They were also supposed to mix through the crowd to invite and urge people to join in the competitions with their pet.

Since Derek was involved in meeting and greeting people at the door, as well as putting on a short program for the attendees and any press, he didn't have a chance to closely supervise what Sally was doing. He wasn't initially concerned because everyone seemed to be having a good time and the competitions went off well with plenty of participants. However, the company sold only a few products, and he later learned from another employee that while she was mixing in the crowd, Sally was talking to people about her nutritional supplements and handing out flyers and her own business cards so interested attendees could contact her after the party. This news was very upsetting to Derek, and he wasn't sure what to do next.

What Should Derek Do?

In Derek's place, what would you do and why? What do you think the outcomes of these different options would be? Here are some possibilities:

➲ Fire Sally immediately. She should know without anyone having to tell her that an employee shouldn't promote his or her own business when doing PR for an employer.

➲ Don't rock the boat. Sally has been doing a good job, and this is just a single special event.

➲ Have a meeting for all employees and go over the company's policies about when it is acceptable to work on an outside job or business and when it is not.

➲ Have a private meeting with Sally in which you explain why it was wrong to do PR for her own business at your event, and that you expect Sally to refrain from doing this in the future.

➲ Bawl Sally out for doing her own PR instead of your PR. Point out that she was supposed to assist with selling, but because she didn't sales were minimal, so you are docking her pay a few hundred dollars as a penalty for this.

➲ Check on the extent to which Sally has been pitching her products to other employees while on the job, in order to build your case against Sally.

➲ Other?

In this case, Derek decided to keep Sally on, after getting feedback from his other employees and giving Sally a strong reprimand for her actions. Sally was very apologetic and assured Derek this would never happen again. This is a situation where you could reasonably fire Sally for promoting her own business on your dime. She was not only using your event to do her own business, but wasn't promoting and selling your own products, which could have been a major factor in your slim sales for the event. Then, too, there is the potential for her self-promotion to turn off your customers, because she is pushing a product on them that has nothing to do with the purpose of the celebration. They know she is working for you, so her promotional efforts can reflect badly on your reputation if they are put off by her approach. Additionally, Sally is not a new employee with relatively little experience whom you might expect not to know what to do in different situations. Rather, Sally has been doing fairly high-level PR work. Someone at that level should know what is expected of her. In particular, they should know that the PR code of ethics requires anyone doing PR to put their own employer's interests first and foremost. The fact that another employee reported on her activities shows that they knew it was wrong and wanted you to know this.

Thus, Sally's activities do rise to a fireable offense, although you might take into consideration other factors to help you decide what to do. One way is to get further feedback from other employees, preferably through one-on-one private meetings, to learn what they think of her performance. If they speak highly of her work, confirming your own assessment of Sally's past performance, you might consider giving her another chance. But couple this with a frank discussion in which you tell her what she did was not acceptable and give her a warning that a future transgression will mean immediate termination. Further, clarify your policies about keeping her outside business activities off the job, and set firm limits on using the phone or copy machine for outside activities. Point out that for occasional emergencies this is okay, but not as a regular practice. Alternatively, if the other employees raise serious concerns about Sally's performance or report that she has been frequently engaged in outside calls, copying, or other second-job activities on the job, that's all the more support for firing her.

If you do decide to fire her, make it very clear why her personal promotional work was totally inappropriate and follow that up with a written memo, just in case you need some written documentation should Sally dispute her firing. Be sure to follow any termination policies in your contract with her or whatever is standard in the industry, such as paying her for the time on the job—including the time put in at the party—and giving her final severance pay so she has no grounds for challenging you. Such protection is especially necessary in this case. Sally has already betrayed your trust with her actions. She might challenge her firing, knowing she isn't going to get a good recommendation from you and figuring she has nothing to lose.

Today's Take-Aways

☑ If an employee brings outside activities onto the job, it's a good reason for putting that employee outside.

☑ Once an employee betrays you by participating in outside activities on the job that damage your business, it's time to do some damage control and get rid of whatever caused the damage— namely, your employee.

☑ Don't let employees create their own policies for doing outside activities because they may do more than you want them to on the job. Give them some guidelines for what you will allow.

☑ When you feel an employee is doing good work and your other employees agree, a firm reprimand often will bring a good employee back in line.

Part V

Communication

Communication Breakdown

Sometimes you think you are communicating what you want, but an employee who thinks he or she understands really doesn't. If that employee assures you he or she knows what to do, you may believe everything's being handled successfully, only to find that the work is done incorrectly—or not at all. What can make this worse is when you have an employee who is working independently, such as an outside salesperson or PR person whom you can't supervise closely. And if that employee is the type of person who likes to take the initiative—a great plus if the employee knows what he or she is doing and does it well—all is well. If they're not, it's a prescription for misunderstandings and conflict.

That's what happened when Maria hired Bettina to do some outside sales and PR for her small business consulting company. Maria was trying to promote her services by setting up speaking engagements and seminar programs for business associations and conventions, both to bring in income and to generate client leads. Plus, she wanted to set up programs and events to which she planned to invite members of the business community as still another way to attract potential clients. She hired Bettina to do various kinds of tasks with different types of payment arrangements, which she made clear at the outset: straight commissions for setting up speaking engagements and seminars by contacting corporations directly, and an hourly rate to help Maria contact speaking bureaus and meeting planners, and create a database of business leads.

At first, everything seemed to be going well. Bettina was working at company headquarters making phone calls, sending out e-mails, putting together the database, and creating a filing system for the different types of contacts and their level of interest. She also carefully documented her hours and what she did, which pleased Maria, who paid her each week for what she did. At the same time, she approached corporate prospects directly on her own time, keeping her own records about who she contacted and their level of interest.

Problems developed when Bettina was clipped by a car and had to spend several weeks at home recuperating for a broken leg. Since Bettina told Maria she had been coming home from seeing a corporate prospect when the accident occurred, Maria felt some responsibility for supporting Bettina with work as best she could through her recovery, even though Bettina was working on a commission-independent contractor basis for any outside sales. So Maria agreed that Bettina could do some of the follow-up work she usually did in the office at home, as well as make corporate calls. "And we'll have the same payment arrangement," Maria told Bettina. "Just let me know what you are doing." Unfortunately, the recovery took longer than expected, so instead of three weeks, it took about two months for Bettina to be up and around again.

Meanwhile, during this time, Bettina did little to tell Maria what she was doing. Mostly she just informed Maria about her prognosis, and after awhile, Maria thought that Bettina wasn't up to working for her, so she herself began to do much of the contact work that Bettina had started.

Finally, after about two months, Bettina called to tell Maria she was now able to get around on her own, so she could come back to work. "Oh, and by the way," she added, "I'll have the billing for you for my hours."

Hours? Maria was flabbergasted, not thinking that Bettina had been doing anything, because Bettina hadn't given her any report of what she had done or the results. At first, she protested that she didn't know Bettina had been able to work during this time and that much of the work Bettina was doing was on a commission basis. But Bettina was adamant: "You told me to keep track of my hours and said you would pay me for any work I did." Then, later that day, Bettina sent in her bill for about 20 hours of work at $20 an hour, listing in general terms what she had done—sending e-mails, making phone calls, and making more follow-up calls.

Maria was outraged. She felt that Bettina was trying to take advantage of her by claiming a payment was due when Maria didn't even know what she had done, asserting she was working on an hourly basis based on what she claimed Maria promised her. This wasn't at all what Maria had told her, so Maria felt unsure what to do. To pay her in full felt like giving in to extortion, yet she feared the repercussions of paying nothing. She wondered if maybe there was some basis for Bettina's misinterpreting what she had said, although she felt she had been very clear, particularly in asking Bettina to keep her informed about what she was doing.

What Should Maria Do?

In Maria's place, what would you do and why? What do you think the outcomes of these different options would be? Here are some possibilities:

- ⮑ Tell Bettina you don't owe her anything because she didn't report on what she was doing as she had when she had worked for you on an hourly basis. You didn't know what she was doing for you or what the results were.

- ⮑ Tell Bettina you don't owe her anything because you were paying on a commission basis for what she was doing.

- ⮑ Ask Bettina for a more complete breakdown of her claimed hours and what she was doing; then pay her for those claimed hours that actually were hourly work.

- ⮑ Tell Bettina there was obviously a communication breakdown. You didn't know that she was working for you, because she didn't keep you informed for two months, and you thought much of her work was on a commission basis. But in the interest of compromise, you will pay her half of what she has billed you.

- ⮑ Agree to pay Bettina what she is asking because it isn't that much, but then terminate her from further employment. She clearly misunderstood your proposed arrangements while she was recovering and didn't keep you informed, which is basic when an employee expects to be paid for her work.

➲ Other?

In this case, Maria actually did work out a compromise payment arrangement and then terminated Bettina from further employment because of the big communication snafu. In a conversation with Bettina the day after she got the bill and had calmed herself down, she told her employee that there was obviously a misunderstanding. Maria told Bettina she would be willing to pay her in full for the activities she did for which she had previously paid her on an hourly basis—the follow-up e-mails to speaking bureaus and meeting planners Bettina had previously contacted—even though Bettina didn't let her know what she was doing. But for everything else, she would pay her half because she had expected Bettina to do that work on a commission basis, as she had before her accident. And then Maria simply didn't ask Bettina to come back and do any more work. In response, Bettina apologized for any misunderstanding and quietly accepted the payment Maria offered, and that was that. Bettina looked for another job while Maria looked for and found another employee to do the outside sales and PR Bettina had been doing.

This seems to have been a good resolution because not paying anything could have left Bettina resentful and hostile, thinking that Maria had discounted what she understood Maria had told her. On the other hand, to pay her in full would have left Maria feeling taken advantage of, particularly since she had tried to make special accommodations for Bettina to work for her while she was recovering at home. Instead, Maria found a compromise that could have been either a straight 50 percent down the middle, or the slightly additional amount that Maria paid by being able to identify when Bettina was doing work for which Maria had paid her in full before. This additional amount was especially fair, because Bettina hadn't kept her informed about what she was doing as she had in the past. Perhaps this fairness contributed to Bettina's willingness to accept Maria's proposed payment compromise without any further efforts to negotiate more.

Finally, Maria was completely justified in not rehiring Bettina because her lack of communication about what she was doing for payment for two months was so egregious. After all, outside employees regularly expect to keep employers informed, normally on a weekly or daily basis. Even a bi-weekly basis might be acceptable. But to not communicate for two months and then expect payment for hours spent when an employer has no idea that one is working for them is not reasonable.

Today's Take-Aways

☑ If outside employees don't tell you what they are doing for an extended period of time, it may be time to tell them you've heard enough and it's time for them to go.

☑ Sometimes you really are being perfectly clear and an employee just doesn't get it. If so, after a time, it's time to get rid of that employee.

☑ A good way to resolve many misunderstandings is with a compromise, where you each give a little even if you know you were very clear and were still misunderstood.

30

What Are You Talking About?

Sometimes a big problem is communicating with employees doing specialized work who literally speak a different language—not a foreign language, but a kind of techno-babble that you simply don't understand. Such employees will often use that language to conceal and misdirect when they have done something wrong. Their specialized language makes it hard to know what they are talking about for anyone outside their field; it's like you need a translator or have to be one in order to clarify what they are doing or have done. And in the process you may not realize that something is going wrong—and they may not want you to know.

That's the situation Kevin, a project manager for a large software development company, faced with Curt, who worked under him as a senior software developer. Curt was in charge of a group of software developers working on security systems and medical equipment. The problem was that Curt would either talk in detailed technical language or would be very vague, so it was hard for Kevin to know what was going on and whether the project was progressing smoothly. Kevin described the situation this way: "As project manager, I'm involved in liaison with both the sales and marketing department and the technical department, conveying to the software developers what customers want and then keeping sales and marketing informed about how things are going."

However, Kevin often had trouble knowing what the developers were doing, particularly when they ran into snags and there were delays. As he explained, "Whenever I spoke to Curt about what the developers were working on or what problem was causing a delay, he would be very indirect and vague. When I tried to get him to be more specific, he would talk in code, using all kinds of technical terms, so I didn't really know what he was talking about. But then, if I pulled it up on the computer to see a visual, I would see what he was talking about and it would make sense."

This use of tech-speak was also a problem when Kevin set up a meeting with the sales and marketing team so they could learn about the product in order to sell it or could explain to their clients why the product was taking longer or costing more than expected. As Kevin noted, "Curt would go off on tangents in describing what the developers were working on. When I would step in to try to stop him and get him to focus and clarify, he wouldn't answer the question. Instead, he would answer some other question that wasn't even asked. He was like a politician who didn't want to answer a particular question, either because he didn't know the answer and didn't want others to know he didn't know, or he didn't want to admit there was a problem that had come up in the project. So he would try to confuse his listeners by using language that was either very vague, or very specific and technical. And when he was called on that he wouldn't answer or he would give some other non-relevant answer."

Likewise, Kevin found it difficult to pin Curt down about whether there could be any danger in using a new software product they had designed. As Kevin explained, "There's often a great deal of pressure in launching products and meeting schedules, so people want to avoid acknowledging potential problems. It can also be difficult to tell how serious a potential problem could be, because it may seem hypothetical until the product is actually used in the field and someone gets hurt. So that's another time when Curt will talk in such a way that it's hard to understand him. He's trying to avoid acknowledging any problems that might delay the schedule for launching products or damage his reputation or that of others on his team." Then, too, if problems were revealed, peoples' jobs might be on the line and a person might be asked to leave.

So Kevin felt in a bind because he was supposed to present an accurate picture to the sales and marketing people of how development was proceeding, as well as make determinations about when products were ready for the market. He felt frustrated in trying to talk to Curt, since he was so hard to understand. But Kevin felt it was an integral part of his job as project manager to understand Curt in order to understand what Curt was doing.

What Should Kevin Do?

In Kevin's place, what would you do and why? What do you think the outcomes of these different options would be? Here are some possibilities for what to do:

⊃ Complain to your own boss, who is in charge of all the different divisions in the company, about Curt's performance as the software development manager; maybe your boss will replace Curt with someone else.

⊃ Tell Curt that he needs to be clearer in what he tells you about what his team is doing, or you need to speak to someone else in his department to explain things. If he refuses, tell him you will speak to the head boss in charge of all the different company divisions.

⊃ Continue to use Curt's initial comments as a general guide; then check on what Curt is saying by looking at visuals so you better understand. Curt clearly needs someone to translate from tech-speak for him.

⊃ Ask Curt to set up a meeting for you with the whole software development division so everyone can explain what they are doing, because Curt is unable to articulate this himself.

⊃ Discuss with your own boss the danger of launching products before they are ready in order to meet schedules. Ask him to talk directly to Curt about not doing this and not being forthright about whether products are really ready.

⊃ Other?

In today's high-tech world, communication between technical employees and others can be a growing problem. Linguistic styles are so different, and high-tech employees who otherwise do a good job aren't good at communicating what they do to others. In some cases, they may have an ulterior motive to obscure what they are doing—such as when there are delays or other problems on projects—but in other cases, they simply have difficulty communicating.

Since one of your jobs as project manager is acting as a liaison between the tech department and marketing, sales, and others in the company, it is probably best to do what you can to act as a translator. For example, continue to look at the visuals for the project to help you understand, using Curt's initial comments as a general guide. Or ask Curt to bring others working on a project in to a meeting to help explain what Curt cannot. Still another approach is to reflect back what you think the other person is trying to tell you, and let them confirm whether you are correct or not and what, if anything, you have wrong. Then try to modify what the other person says is incorrect. You should get increasingly closer using this technique, until you finally get it right.

Although Curt may be skilled in guiding his team, his problem is clearly communicating what the team is doing. Do what you can to help the process, without putting him on the defensive by accusing him of deliberately trying to obscure information on the project. Give him the benefit of the doubt that it's just a communication problem, unless you have reason to believe there may be problems on the project contributing to Curt's desire to keep things muddy.

If you do feel there may be problems, try being supportive as a way to get Curt or others on his team to explain what's really going on. For example, point out that you understand the pressures of trying to get out software to meet a deadline, but it's more important to bring out software that works and avoid any possible dangers, such as could happen to patients in the case of medical software. Point out that you will go to bat for the software development team in seeking to explain why the development group needs more time or resources to properly develop the software. This way, they will come to see you as their advocate rather than an opponent representing the marketing and sales people. Then Curt and the others will be more likely to level with you as best they can. Additionally, you can use your knowledge of what's really going on to talk to your own boss and others in the company about when the software will be ready, along with the pitfalls of releasing it out before it is.

In this case, Kevin combined aspects of all of the above methods to overcome the language barrier between him and Curt, and the improved communication helped the company, too.

Today's Take-Aways

☑ If trying to get information and clarification directly doesn't work, try some alternate ways of getting that information, such as using visuals or asking others who are better communicators to give you input, too.

☑ Think of geek-speak as another language that not everyone can translate. Then do what you can to translate it yourself, or bring in a translator to do that for you.

☑ Try acting as a reflecting mirror or echo to describe back what you think you understand, and let the other person keep correcting you, until you get your understanding right.

Silence Is Golden

Not every employee makes a good team player or is a good communicator. In fact, an inarticulate, hard-to-talk-to employee can sometimes be very effective and productive in the right setting. But in the wrong place, he or she can seem like the employee from hell. It's all a matter of context, and the right kind of management can make the difference.

That's what happened when Shauna was transferred into a public relations and information management office for a company that handled corporate communications and customer relations. She found that most of the employees, a half-dozen women in their 20s and 30s, had joined together into a tightly knit group that not only worked together well on the job, but also socialized and partied together off the job. But one woman, 20-year-old Maureen, stayed completely outside the circle. Maureen had joined the company as a college intern and was still involved in a college internship program that paid her a small stipend, substantially less than anyone else. Even so, she said she liked the work and wanted to learn about PR.

Maureen did a good job when given clear direction, such as typing up material or entering information into a database. She also was very reliable and prompt in coming to work. But she constantly was in the middle of some kind of an uproar. Some of the women accused her of typing up the wrong cards they had given her to type.

Others asked her to make changes in the databases she was updating, but she entered the data in the wrong file. Another woman asked Maureen to prepare a boilerplate contract, and Maureen wrote up the contract and terms information incorrectly. When one of the employees confronted her about it, Maureen simply said quietly, almost in a whisper, "This is what they told me to do," referring to the counselor who originally assigned the project to her.

When the company had its Christmas holiday party, Maureen seemed very uncooperative. Assigned to help out at the reception table, Maureen looked glum and unfriendly, and seemed to frown when she greeted new people and told them to fill out a nametag. By contrast, the two women she worked with at the table were constantly making small talk and winning over the attendees.

Shauna asked Maureen to come into her office to discuss what was going on. Maureen seemed so reticent and closed off that Shauna felt uncomfortable talking to her. Maureen answered her questions in just a few words: "Yes . . . No . . . That's okay . . . Yes, I'll do that . . . Whatever you think." And when she wanted Maureen to give her an opinion on something, such as telling her what kind of job she would prefer to do, Maureen wouldn't offer one, saying something like, "I don't know" or "Either one is okay." Shauna even tried to get Maureen to relax by asking her about how she liked school and what her plans for the future were, and Maureen's answers were almost monosyllabic: "It's okay" and "I don't know."

At the end of the meeting, Shauna felt very frustrated and ready to terminate Maureen because she was making so many mistakes, and because she brought into the office a sense of gloom and doom that bothered the other employees. Shauna herself felt unnerved trying to get Maureen to communicate, likening the experience to pulling hardened taffy out of a box. Yet Maureen was also in an internship program, and Shauna was concerned that firing Maureen would prevent her from getting college credit for a class she needed for her school, thus making it harder for her to find employment in the future.

What Should Shauna Do?

In Shauna's place, what would you do and why? What do you think the outcomes of these different options would be? Here are some possibilities:

➲ Fire Maureen, regardless of the internship agreement. She obviously doesn't fit in a company that does PR.

➲ Insist that Maureen has to be more of a team player if she wants to stay in the company.

➲ Assign one of the women to be Maureen's mentor and to help her become more of team player.

➲ Give Maureen some work she can do on her own and give her very clear directions, along with samples of what to do. She is obviously very shy and would do better in tasks where she doesn't have to interact with others.

➲ Have a meeting with the other members of the department and Maureen so everyone can air their complaints about Maureen.

➲ Don't feel you have to be responsible for Maureen's lack of fit in the company. Maureen needs to learn now where she fits in and where she doesn't.

➲ Other?

The basic problem here is that Maureen is extremely reticent and shy, and she needs more direction to do a good job. She does seem to have good potential because she is reliable and prompt, but has run into problems in working with other staff members. She seems to feel uncomfortable with them and interacting with others, such as when she is assigned to meet and greet at a reception table. In turn, she may feel out of place working with the other staff members because of the great difference between her and their personality and style; she may also be confused by the lack of clarity and support she has gotten from them when they have given her assignments. Then, too, she seems to lack the confidence to think for herself or share an opinion, and pushing her has only seemed to force her to withdraw further into her shell, behavior that is reflected in the very short and tentative replies.

So what to do? Under the circumstances, it is probably best not to try to push her to adapt to the more outgoing group of employees who have formed their own close circle because she already feels like the outsider. In turn, they have made it clear they feel uncomfortable around her and would rather have her gone. Rather, what might work best is to find some work that she feels comfortable doing on her own and giving her some clear direction for doing it so she can shine.

Maybe down the road, as she acquires more confidence in what she is doing, she may begin to become more outgoing and assertive. For now, start with where she is and work with that.

And that is exactly what Shauna did. She found a small office where Maureen could work quietly typing documents and entering data, and sometimes she gave her small prototypes for presentations to make. In these circumstances, Maureen thrived. Once she knew precisely what to do, she didn't need much supervision, and she worked quickly and productively. Shauna felt a little awkward at first, dispensing with the ordinary small talk she engaged in with other employees, such as asking about their weekend or sharing comments on the weather and local news. But Maureen seemed to do just fine without such chit chat. Instead, each morning when Maureen arrived at work, Shauna simply reviewed the work she would be doing that day and gave her any needed materials, or pointed her to the current database file she would be working on. Then Maureen went to work through the day, with very few breaks. She liked working alone in her own little world. By finding Maureen's comfort zone and not pushing further, Shauna turned what had been a problem employee into one who was very productive and a great contributor to the team in her own private way. In fact, Maureen came to work for the company following the completion of her internship program.

Today's Take-Aways

- ☑ Finding more suitable work can sometimes turn a problem employee into a productive one.
- ☑ While training, coaching, and mentoring can certainly help many employees, sometimes all you need to do is find work an employee is good at and likes to do and then close the door.
- ☑ If you've got a round peg, it may help to find a round hole for it, rather than try to re-cut the peg as a square one to fit into a square hole.
- ☑ If you can start where an employee is at, that may be a good starting point for reshaping and training that employee later.

Who's in Charge Here?

One dilemma in getting rid of a bad employee is not being sure who is responsible for firing that employee. As a result, the termination process can take much longer than usual. It may even take longer to realize that you have a problem employee, when the chain of command and communication is diffused and uncertain. Still more complications can arise if the employee is in possession of critical information that you need to get back.

That's the situation faced by Michael, a minister who headed a small church under the auspices of a board of directors, a hiring committee, and a group of volunteers. Michael had hired Martha as a part-time bookkeeper to keep the books, send out the payroll checks to the church's staff of five employees, and pay the church's bills. Martha was hired after the minister of another church across the street recommended her to the hiring committee; he referred her because someone in his church mentioned that she had been freelancing as a bookkeeper for a number of organizations. Since another minister had recommended her and the hiring committee went along with his recommendation, Michael just conducted a brief interview with her and dispensed with doing a more extensive background check or asking for references. He figured, if she's good enough for the other minister and the hiring committee, she's good enough for me.

Initially, Martha was supposed to come to the church to work on the books, payrolls, and bills. But after a couple of weeks of setting up the system, she suggested that she could work more efficiently at her computer at home; she had the latest Quicken software and the church's software was about five years old. So she took the computerized records home on a CD, along with the church's record books, and then entered the data on her own computer.

Everything seemed fine until it turned out Martha wasn't working at home writing the payroll checks and paying the bills. However, no one knew for about six weeks that there was a problem. Then the church got a notice that the phone was about to be shut off if the bill wasn't paid within ten days. And then the secretary asked why she hadn't received her payroll check. She hadn't asked earlier because she was afraid of appearing "money hungry" in a church that valued helping and being of service to others.

Suddenly, Michael, the hiring committee, and board of directors realized they had a problem, but the lines of authority in the church were muddled. Michael paid the phone bill to prevent a cut-off in service, but he wasn't sure what to do about the situation. Martha now had the latest church records on her computer; he didn't want to fire her until he got all the records back from her. This might require getting newer software in order to be able to read whatever she had added to the original records. Plus, he wasn't sure who had the authority to actually fire her. The hiring committee had been involved in the original hiring process, the church treasurer signed her check, and the board of directors made overall decisions affecting church business, which meant its members should provide input into the situation, too. Additionally, he wanted to find out why she wasn't doing the job, as she had been hired on the recommendation of another minister with the approval of the hiring committee.

Ultimately, the entire process took about three months, including a month spent diplomatically asking for and getting the records back from Martha, who explained apologetically that she hadn't had time to get out the checks. Why? Because apparently she was trying to manage a dozen freelance jobs—from house-sitting, to walking dogs, to handling several bookkeeping accounts for different clients. She just had too many irons in the fire, so she kept putting off doing the books for the church. And then, after Michael and the committee realized she had to go, they had to clarify who could fire her—the minister, the church treasurer, or the hiring committee. Ultimately, it was decided that the minister could fire her, and so Michael did, trying to do so as gently as possible, because he didn't want to seem like the "bad guy," even though everyone agreed she had to go.

What Should Michael Have Done and What Should He Do in the Future?

Clearly, this was a difficult, murky situation. But is there anything Michael might have done differently, or could do in the future to avoid such a mess. In Michael's place, what would you do and why? What do you think the outcomes of these different options would be? Here are some possibilities:

➲ Have regular meetings with everyone involved in the hiring and firing process so you can go over recent hires and discuss how they are working out.

➲ Establish a probationary period for all new employees, even those working part-time.

➲ Set up organizational policies and procedures, so you know who has the authority to both hire and fire employees.

➲ When someone makes a recommendation or referral to you, find out what they know about the person they are recommending or referring. They may not really know the quality of the person's work themselves.

➲ Do a background check, including a check for references—even if you have a recommendation or referral—for the reasons noted above.

➲ .Don't let someone working for you outside of your physical premises have the only working copy of important records; stay in charge of them yourself.

➲ Have a person working outside your organization provide a short weekly report so you know what he or she is doing.

➲ Other?

One of the big problems with hiring Martha in the first place was the laxness of the hiring process. Michael and the hiring committee literally took on faith the referral from the minister of the other church. In fact, the other minister knew little about Martha, apart from someone in his church mentioning that she did freelance book-keeping work.

Thus, there should have been some more careful screening, in-cluding references from previous clients and questions about why she had so many part-time and temporary jobs. Sure, freelancing can result in doing good work on lots of short-time jobs. But it can also be a cover-up for someone leaving a number of jobs because of poor performance. Check on the person's background, so it doesn't end up biting you on the backside.

Additionally, Michael should not let critical information about the organization out the door. Such information, dealing with highly confidential documents, is better done within the organization to keep control over it and reduce possibility of it being leaked out in today's highly porous information age. And even if it made sense to release this information to someone thought to be a trusted party, Michael should have made sure the church office had a back-up copy. There's simply no excuse in this day of CD copiers and DVD burners not to make this extra copy. If there's a problem of software compatibility, it's important that you either upgrade to the current version, or have your own records saved in an earlier version format so you can still access these records yourself. In the event you have a falling out with an employee working offsite, you then have this critical information and your work won't be held up while you work out any arrangements to terminate the employee.

Michael also might have had an initial probationary period or set one up for the future, because this is a good way to put a new employee on notice that he or she will be subject to extra supervision and reporting in the first few weeks. Then, Michael could have used this time to check that Martha had not only set up a system, but also was actually using it to send out payroll checks and pay bills. He didn't have one in this instance, but he definitely should establish such a procedure in the future.

However, it may not be necessary to have large organizational meetings to assess how employees are doing and review any sugges-tions for termination. In fact, such a meeting can slow down and overly burden the process, particularly when this is a meeting of people or subgroups with relatively similar levels of power and decision making responsibilities, such as with a minister, hiring commit-tee, and board of directors, in contrast to a boss-staff meeting. The range of input can seriously slow down the consideration process and isn't necessary for evaluating relatively low-level employee deci-sions, such as whether to hire or fire a bookkeeper. Rather, as was decided at Michael's church through multiple meetings, he had the power to do this all along. It should have been clear he had this power all along—and that he has this power in the future.

Today's Take-Aways

☑ Just like at sea, you need clear channels of command and com-munication. Otherwise when it comes to making a decision about hiring and firing, you could be at sea.

☑ Don't turn over critical information you need to run your busi-ness to a part-time outside employee you have just hired—or worse, end up not having this information yourself. It's like giv-ing away the keys to your house and then not keeping a copy for yourself.

☑ Don't just let an outside recommendation or referral determine who you hire; do some independent checking to make sure you agree with what the outsiders say.

☑ Don't just have faith—even in a church—that a new employee, particularly one working outside your organization, knows what he or she is doing. Back up your faith with some form of feed-back and forms.

When the Cat's Away

Even a company owner or manager needs some time off and should be able to count on their supervisors or employees to do the work in their absence, make reasonable decisions, and keep them informed about important developments. But problems can develop when the employee left in charge is irresponsible and doesn't do what is necessary to keep the business running effectively—or takes on responsibilities and makes decisions that are counter-productive for the business. Even worse can be when an employee conceals critical information from the business owner or manager, leading to costly repairs and corrections as a result of the gap.

That's what happened for Cheri and Brad, who ran a thriving boat sales and rental store. They had been running the shop for several years, working 60- and 70-hour weeks, to build up their business, and now they felt they needed a vacation because they hadn't had one in years. They just had to take some time for themselves. And they felt the business now was at a point where they could step away briefly and leave operations in the hands of their employees, most of whom had been with them for over two years.

Thus, at a staff meeting, they explained the situation, invited employees who were interested in coordinating operations while they were gone to let them know, and then interviewed the few employees who volunteered to decide who should be in charge. The result was that they selected two employees, Betsy and Jerry, to take over management while they were away. They gave them some extra bonuses for doing so, described the arrangements at the next staff meeting before they left, and found the rest of the staff highly supportive. After the staff threw them a going-away party, they flew to France and then to sunny Italy, where they spent a glorious two weeks. Just in case, the employees had their cell phone number to reach them for emergencies, but no one called them. They were glad, feeling like the employees had been up to successfully managing the business themselves in their absence.

However, soon after Cheri and Brad returned, they discovered Betsy and Jerry had made a completely inappropriate decision and had not told them critical information that proved very costly. "It would have taken only a simple phone call to ask for our input or tell us what was happening at the time," Cheri complained. "Then they didn't even tell us what had happened when we came back, which ended up costing us thousands of dollars in lost business and damages to our operations."

As Cheri and Brad explained, the first problem came when Betsy and Jerry decided to change their regular operating hours of 8 a.m. to 8 p.m. on Friday to 8 a.m. to 6 p.m. because it was summer and the employees wanted to leave early for the weekend. While the change might have been popular with the employees, it resulted in some lost customers who came to the shop only to find it closed. Plus, there were complaints from others who wanted to return a boat they had leased for a work event, only to find they couldn't do so. "That isn't a decision that employees should make," Brad pointed out. "That's a management policy and prerogative to set hours. The employees were thinking of themselves, not the customers, when they made the change, and they didn't even call to check with us for our approval."

But the second problem was even more serious. While they were gone, the computer crashed, so Betsy and Jerry turned everything off to start the computer again. The computer was now running on the back-up system, although Betsy and Jerry didn't realize this and they didn't even tell Cheri and Brad about the crash when they returned. As a result, about a month later, when the computer crashed again, over three months of data was lost, which included information on sales, customers, payroll, promotional materials, and more.

It turned out to be about a $20,000 mistake. What also disturbed Cheri and Brad is the two employees who had coordinated operations in their absence didn't feel they were responsible, because the second crash had occurred after Cheri and Brad had been back for several weeks. "They claimed that they weren't responsible since it happened on our watch, and they didn't think it necessary to bother us on our vacation about the first computer crash, because the computer was quickly up and running again. So everything seemed back to normal, and they didn't understand that it would only *appear* this way because the computer was running on back-up. They didn't recognize that they should have told us about the crash either while we were away or after our return. Then we could have had a computer person come in and install an additional back-up system after the first one had failed, so we wouldn't have lost any data."

So now Cheri and Brad were contemplating what to do about the situation.

What Should Cheri and Brad Do?

Should Cheri and Brad hold Betsy and Jerry responsible for their bad decisions or not? Should they penalize them in any way? And what should they do to prevent such a problem in the future? In Cheri and Brad's place, what would you do and why? What do you think the outcomes of these different options would be? Here are some possibilities:

➲ Let it go and suck up the loss. Betsy and Jerry were just filling in as managers. They didn't realize shutting the shop two hours early was wrong, and they didn't think the first computer crash was significant because the computer started up again.

➲ Talk to Betsy and Jerry and explain that you don't plan to take any punitive action against them, as they didn't know what type of decisions required management approval and what type of information was important to share. Then explain why they should have asked for your input and told you what happened.

➲ Dock the wages of Betsy and Jerry, because they caused you $20,000 in losses by not telling you about the first computer crash.

➲ Fire Betsy and Jerry. They not only caused you $20,000 in losses by not telling you about the first computer crash, but they refused to accept responsibility for not telling you about this crash, which led to your devastating data loss when the second crash occurred.

➲ Let it go and don't rock the boat. Betsy and Jerry have been productive, loyal employees for over two years and they were only filling in for you on a part-time basis. This will show you value initiative and encourage other employees to step up to the plate.

➲ Other?

While Betsy and Jerry may have made a bad decision and failed to tell you important information, they have been good employees in the past, and they did step up to the plate in offering to take care of the office for you while you were on vacation. As first-time temporary managers, they also might not have been clear about what they could decide on themselves and what they needed to tell you. They also might not have understood enough about computers and back-up systems to realize that while the computer was working fine, it was doing so on the back-up system. And they might have been trying to do what they could themselves so you could enjoy your vacation.

Thus, it is understandable why they might not feel they were responsible for making a bad decision in closing the office early on two days when they had the support of the employees to do so, and why they might not feel the subsequent crash is their responsibility. While their actions might have led to losses due to their bad decision and failure to tell you critical information, their actions could be seen as reasonable under the circumstances. Moreover, since they have been good employees in the past, temporarily took on additional responsibilities, and had the best of intentions in managing in your absence, it might be best to not take any punitive actions against them. Doing so might serve as a warning to other employees not to take the initiative and not to take on more responsibilities themselves.

Have a discussion with Betsy and Jerry, assuring them that you are not taking any punitive action against them. Explain why certain types of decisions should be approved by you and why certain type of information should be given to you. Then, for the future, develop some protocols and have a discussion with the staff as a whole so everyone is briefed on what to do should you be away from the office for a few days or weeks in the future. Include a section on what to do about the circumstances that caused your problems this time (i.e., these are your hours, and don't make any changes without your approval; this is how the computer system is set up, so it is important to advise you if there are any malfunctions). But also detail other policies and procedures, and try to anticipate any future scenarios the employees might face in your absence so you can detail what to do.

In short, in some circumstances, you may think an employee is being difficult when the employee is simply making mistakes when they take on additional responsibilities and unfamiliar tasks that they really don't know how to do. Cheri and Brad chalked this up as an educational experience, giving them insights on what to do to prepare employees for better decision making and information sharing in the future.

Today's Take-Aways

- ☑ When you encourage an employee to take on more responsibilities, recognize that an employee can make mistakes. Don't penalize an employee for the first one because this might discourage all your employees from taking on more responsibilities.

- ☑ Just because you think an employee is being difficult, this isn't always the case; it may be the employee needs more information and guidance in order to do the job well.

- ☑ When things go wrong, think of ways to make changes and corrections in the future; it could be an educational moment to help you do things differently and better.

- ☑ When employees make bad decisions, think of how to help them make better decisions in the future. When employees don't tell you what you think you should know, help the employees better know what they need to tell you.

Putting the Customer First

In today's competitive marketplace, putting the customer first has become a mantra. The goal is to get loyal customers—sometimes called "raving fans"—not just satisfied customers who can easily be enticed away by other companies. Lots of attention is paid to customer service to provide that competitive edge, and employees are awarded for going the extra mile to help the customer. This can be a great approach, except when an employee takes it too far, such as running up costs in the name of customer service. Unfortunately, some employees may do this because they are so concerned with garnering customer appreciation and affection that they forget about doing what's best for the business. In that case, going the extra mile turns into taking a very long hike, to the detriment of the business.

That's what happened for Charlie, who ran a pet store. He had an employee, Jen, who would go to all extremes to help the client, even if it was bad for the business. In one case, the store had a client who asked for a special pet food for her dog, not the usual packaged dog food. Jen took her order and assured her that they would have the pet food ready for her to pick up the following day around noon. Then, the store got very busy, and in the rush of customers, many bringing along their pets which added to the chaos, Jen forgot to order the special food.

The matter could have been resolved by a simple apology to the long-time customer; maybe even with an extra bag of food or an extra discount to compensate. But instead of pursuing that alternative and explaining the situation to the customer, Jen, as Charlie put it, "went to the ends of the earth to get it." Since the company's usual vendor wouldn't be able to get it until the following day, Jen began calling around to other retail stores in the area until she located a retailer who stocked the product about 30 miles away, and drove off herself to get a few cans of pet food. The result was that the store was short-staffed for about two hours while she sought the pet food. This left some customers fuming because of the long wait, lost some sales when unhappy customers left rather than wait, and incurred extra expenses for gas and tolls for her long drive.

"Her way of serving the customer just didn't make sense," said Charlie, "and it was hard for her to understand why her extra effort to help the customer wasn't appreciated."

In other cases, Jen would interrupt other salespeople working with customers to get an answer for one of her own customers. "She didn't even wait sometimes. She would just burst in to the middle of a conversation with her question," Charlie complained, "rather than telling the customer with a question that she would find out the information and that it might take a minute or two while she did. That way, she could wait until another salesperson had finished a conversation with a customer or ask the other salesperson to come over to help her with a customer question when he or she was free."

Unfortunately, when Charlie tried to talk to her about her behavior, she became defensive, insisting that she was only trying to help the customers, and the customers loved her as a result. Yes, it may be they did, but she went so far out of her way to help them that her over-the-top customer service was costing the company money, and in some cases, her interference with the sales process of other salespeople was losing sales.

Charlie wasn't sure what to do. How could he reach Jen, or should he give up and fire her?

What Should Charlie Do?

The dilemma for Charlie was to find a way to change an employee who was so far resistant to change because she thought she was providing excellent service to the customer, or terminate her employment. If you were in Charlie's place, what would you do and why? What do you think the outcomes of these different options would be? Here are some possibilities:

- ➲ Give up on Jen and tell her you aren't going to take it anymore.
- ➲ Give Jen one more chance, telling her that while you appreciate her gung-ho attitude towards customers, she has to put the needs of the business first.
- ➲ Have a meeting with the employees as a group, and go over the store's policies about how to put the customer first but not go too far.
- ➲ Document the times when Jen has gone overboard in doing too much for customers, and tell her how you expect her to deal with those situations in the future. Then insist that she do it your way, or she will be on her way.
- ➲ Ask a long-time trusted employee who is handling sales along with Jen to keep an eye on what she is doing. That person can either give Jen advice on what to do differently in dealing with a customer or contact you about the problem, so you can step in.
- ➲ Other?

In this case, Jen's problem is not clearly understanding when and how it is appropriate to take extra steps to help the customer and not, along with her resistance to doing things differently. While she may be well-meaning, her customer-first focus is so extreme that she is undermining the business, and either has to be set straight or has to go.

Since she is well-meaning and trying to be helpful, perhaps it might be worth it to give her one more chance, but be very clear about what you expect and what the consequences will be— terminating her employment—if she doesn't change. To that end, a good heart-to-heart talk is in order. Go over the circumstances under which it is appropriate to go the extra mile, and perhaps even write up some examples of situations and what to do. Also detail the circumstances in which it is not appropriate to go above and beyond, and how to handle such cases. Tell her that you really appreciate her concern for the customer, but that she has to temper it with good sense. Her efforts should result in profits for the business rather than costing the business money. Perhaps you could even set up some role plays for her to act out some appropriate responses.

In short, go a little further than before in clarifying what you expect her to do and what you don't want her to do, and emphasize that she has to change if she wants to keep her job. Then, monitor her behavior herself, or ask a trusted employee who works with her to do some of this observation and keep you informed of how Jen is doing.

If you find Jen is doing better, even if there is a slip-up or two, keep working with her and support her in the changes she is making. Perhaps provide her a reward to show you appreciate her changed behavior, such as a small cash bonus; a symbol of recognition, such as a ribbon or plaque presented at a staff meeting; or some other perk. Alternatively, if you find that nothing has changed—or is changing—after a few weeks, it's time to let Jen go. Simply explain that nothing has changed, pay her whatever is due, and wish her well in the future.

In the case at hand, Charlie found Jen quite willing to change her behavior, once he explained that she was costing the business money and sales. He carefully reviewed the times when she had not acted appropriately and specifically mentioned other times when she had. After he helped her see the difference this way, she adjusted her customer service accordingly.

Today's Take-Aways

- ☑ While it's great for an employee to go the extra mile in dealing with customers, don't let the employee take a long hike.

- ☑ While customer service should put the customer first, you need to put the business first if serving a customer's needs becomes too expensive.

- ☑ Help employees understand the importance of serving the business as well as serving the customer.

- ☑ If an employee keeps serving the customer to the detriment of the business, the best way to serve the business is to let that employee go.

Part VI

Putting It All Together

Bad Employee or Bad Boss?

When you have a series of bad employees, your experience may show a pattern in which you make similar complaints about your employees or they make similar complaints about you. As a result, you may be thinking you have problem employees, when the real problem is YOU! This may happen because you are repeating the same mistakes in hiring or making difficult demands that no employee can truly satisfy. Or it may be something about the way you manage that leaves employees in the dark or feeling hostile and resentful, triggering what you view as bad employee behavior.

Employees don't want to recognize that they are at fault and not their boss, and the same is true about bosses who complain about difficult employees. Managers and company owners don't want to see imperfections in themselves. They may find it hard to recognize the situation for what it is because, as psychological researchers have shown, people don't like to blame themselves for their problems. Whether you're an employee or a boss, you generally like to take the credit when something goes well and tend to think the positive outcome is due to your abilities and actions. By contrast, when things go wrong, you would rather put the responsibility outside of yourself and onto others, or blame bad luck in general so you don't have to take the blame.

But if you want to overcome a problem that can seriously hamper your success as a manager or company owner, you have to make an effort to overcome this natural tendency to blame others rather than yourself.

Consider that you may be the problem if you see a continuing pattern of having difficult employees. Sometimes this can manifest itself as conflicts with a number of employees in the workplace. Or it may show up in a history of high turnover or higher-than-usual turnover, because one of the major reasons for employees leaving a job is having a bad boss. Thus, when you find a repeated series of similar problems with employees, take a close look at yourself. Otherwise, you might be unlikely to recognize that you are the main source of the problem or at least a major contributor to it.

Some common problems might be:

- Being a bad communicator, so you leave your employees confused about what to do
- Being unreasonably tough, so your employees feel you are unfair or a tyrant to work for, leaving them unmotivated
- Being too disorganized, so you don't provide your employees with the support they need to be effective

In fact, if you look through the list of problem bosses in my book, *A Survival Guide for Working with Bad Bosses,* you will see the factors that contribute to being a bad boss. One or more of these could be the reason that you are having a series of problems with employees:

- Too aggressive, or too controlling and manipulative
- Not aggressive or controlling enough, or weak and wishy-washy
- Too organized and structured, or too rigid and inflexible
- Too unorganized and/or disorganized, or too uncertain and vacillating
- Too emotional
- Lacking compassion and empathy
- Too much of a micromanager
- Too much of a perfectionist
- Not providing direction or instruction, or being involved in your own projects and not interested in managing

➲ Making impulsive or bad decisions

➲ Indecisive

➲ Too nosy and invasive

➲ Yelling, screaming, and being rude and insulting

➲ Making unwanted sexual advances in the office or becoming involved in a sexual relationship with another employee

➲ Involved in criminal activities and asking employees to cover up or participate in these activities

➲ Lying and failing to keep promises, thus creating an atmosphere of distrust among employees

➲ Unfair, playing office favorites or not giving proper recognition or credit.

Any of these factors can contribute to poor morale, reduced productivity, rebellious or seditious employees, high absenteeism or lateness, high turnover, and other problems. So when you see a pattern of bad employee behavior, even if these are different types of bad behaviors, consider if you have any of these above characteristics that might be contributing to this behavior.

For example, a few people I spoke to at business networking events or met through referrals had a half-dozen or more stories to share where there seemed to be a reason that their employees were acting up—or acting out.

➲ In one case, Edmond repeatedly had employees who didn't measure up to his high standards, resulting in many complaints on his part about lazy, incompetent, and irresponsible employees. But it turned out that he didn't make his requirements fully clear when he hired employees; didn't provide the supportive training and follow-up monitoring the employees needed to know what they were doing; and left employees feeling demoralized when he turned his corrections of mistakes into put-downs rather than providing guidance on what to do to improve performance. In addition, some of his standards seemed overly precise and nitpicky, making it hard for anyone to do exactly what he wanted, particularly when he didn't provide the training and guidance to reach this goal.

⮑   In another case, Lydia was too much of a pushover, so she had many employees who took advantage of her good supportive nature. Because she didn't set clear boundaries, the employees walked over what vague lines she did set. And she retained employees in dysfunctional personal relationships because she felt sorry for them, even though their work—or lack of it—was holding the business back. She repeatedly complained about employees who were late, took overly long lunches, were out for extended periods of time due to claims of illness, didn't meet deadlines, and did poor quality work. But rather than firing employees for cause, putting them on suspension, docking their pay, or otherwise cracking down, she repeatedly gave employees another chance. So they took advantage because she let them until the problems continued to build up and she finally took some action.

⮑   And then there was Judith, who gave the wrong employees too much power and control because of her hands-off management style. She frequently traveled to trade shows and conferences. Without a solid second in command, she left the management in her absence to different employees who weren't skilled in management techniques and weren't accountable, because she didn't have good controls in place. So she didn't really know what the employees were doing. As a result, she had numerous stories of employees who were lying, taking money, treating customers poorly, or in conflict with other employees, because due to her absences or lack of supervision, the employees behaved like a bunch of spoiled kids given too much recess. Eventually, she did fire several employees after she discovered what they had been doing. But if she had better controls, the employees might not have acted out, or she would have caught the serious problems more quickly.

In short, if you do have a pattern of problems with employees, look more closely at yourself and at what you may be doing that is contributing to this employee bad behavior. Or consider the way in which your hiring process might be leading you to hire employees who become problems. Then, think about how you might change this to become a better, stronger boss. To help you do this, write down a list of the employees you have had problems with in one column, note the reasons you had these problems in a second column, and indicate what you might have done yourself that contributed to this situation. Then, notice any recurring themes and ask yourself, "Is there anything I can do to change my own behavior to avoid having these problems in the future?" Consider whatever you write as though it is a management improvement diary. As you identify what you are doing wrong, also include your efforts to improve and chart your progress.

In short, don't just chalk up your problems with employees to the employees themselves, especially when similar problems crop up for different employees. The real problem may not be the employee from hell—it might be you! If so, instead of trying to come up with ways to deal with bad employees, work on fixing yourself because something about your management style is contributing the reasons that you have these difficult employees.

Today's Take-Aways

- ☑ If you have a pattern of problem employees, consider the source of the problem. It may not be the bad employees—it may be you!

- ☑ It may be easier to complain about all the bad employees you have had than to recognize how you have contributed to the problem with your own management style.

- ☑ Just like in nature, when you discover a pattern, if you look more deeply, you can discover the underlying cause creating that pattern—which in this case could be you.

- ☑ Is the problem you, your employee, or both? To fix the problem, you've got to understand it first.

How Bad Is Your Employee (or Employees)?
A Self-Assessment Quiz

How bad is your employee? How difficult is the situation you have to cope with? This quiz will help you rate your situation compared to others so you can better put your own employee or employees in perspective. After all, you may think your employee is really bad in some ways, but not so bad in others, while other managers and company owners may have an employee who is bad in many ways. This quiz will help you better understand what to do to deal with your situation, from talking to your employee to having a staff meeting to issuing clearer instructions to documenting grievances to firing the employee to contacting law enforcement.

These 30 questions are based on the major issues raised in this book. Just rate how bad you think your employee is in each area. Answer as honestly as you can so you can most accurately assess your situation. Understanding is the first step to finding a solution.

Rate your employee or employees on a scale from 0–4 on each question and add up the totals. See the scoring key at the end to see how your employee or team of employees rates.

You'll find that many of these bad behaviors in employees are the same as those used to describe bad bosses (see *A Survival Guide for Working with Bad Bosses*), such as being overly aggressive or too passive, being a poor communicator, being untrustworthy, or committing a crime. Some types of bad behavior cut across lines of power and authority; no matter who does them, they are bad.

	RATING **(from 0–4)**

ATTITUDE
1. My employee is too aggressive in the way he/she deals with me or others in the office; he/she is a bully and is always arguing with me and others. _____
2. My employee is arrogant and insulting to me and others in the office. _____
3. My employee is often insubordinate, standing up to me and acting like he/she knows the best way to do something and I don't. _____
4. My employee doesn't take orders well; he/she often doesn't follow directions or goes off and does the wrong thing on his/her own. _____
5. My employee seems to be mentally unstable or part of a culture of violence and I'm afraid of disciplining or firing him/her. _____
6. My employee is a prima donna who is trying to take charge of and control other employees. _____

COMPETENCE
7. My employee is often incompetent; he/she makes many mistakes, is very disorganized, and has trouble learning how to do the job correctly. _____
8. My employee has claimed to have certain skills, but in fact, doesn't know what he/she doesn't know. _____
9. My employee is a know-it-all who tries to show off and lords it over others in the office, contributing to bad morale. _____

10. My employee is a real slow-poke, taking too
    long to get the job done.   _____
11. My employee is a lazy goof-off, who takes
    lots of time off, including long lunch breaks.   _____
12. My employee can't deal with stress and
    high-pressure situations; he/she can't
    handle multi-tasking, falls apart, and can't
    do the job.

PERSONAL ISSUES

13. My employee is overly sensitive and
    emotional, so it is hard for me or others to
    relate to him/her or correct any poor
    performance.   _____
14. My employee brings all kinds of personal
    problems to the office and these problems
    are interfering with his/her work.   _____
15. My employee is a busybody and gossip who
    pays too much attention to what others are
    doing and talks too much about other
    people, and may even be sharing private
    information about the company or me.   _____
16. My employee has a problem with alcohol or
    drugs.   _____
17. My employee calls in sick a lot.

TRUST AND HONESTY

18. I have caught my employee in a number
    of lies, such as telling lies to cover up
    mistakes, appear better than he/she is, or
    claim to have done something when he/she
    hasn't.   _____
19. My employee has been stealing from the
    company and I have recently caught him/
    her doing this.   _____
20. My employee repeatedly makes promises
    about what he/she will or can do by when,
    but then often doesn't keep these promises.   _____

21. My employee frequently takes credits for others' work, so I think he/she is better than he/she really is. _____

22. I believe my employee is involved in criminal activities off the job. _____

COMMUNICATION

23. My employee acts like he/she understands me, but really doesn't, and then does the work incorrectly. _____

24. My employee is always complaining and griping about everything to others, and it is undermining office morale and everyone's productivity. _____

25. My employee is difficult to talk to and understand because he/she talks in a highly technical language or is vague when he/she tries to explain anything.

INAPPROPRIATE OFFICE BEHAVIOR

26. My employee has been using office equipment and supplies for personal activities and engaging in personal activities on the job. _____

27. My employee has been promoting his/her own business activities to company employees or at company events. _____

28. My employee can't keep a secret and shares confidential information with other employees. _____

29. My employee engages in suggestive comments, staring, joking, groping, or other inappropriate sexual behavior in the workplace, making other employees uncomfortable. _____

30. My employee doesn't get along with other employees; he/she just isn't a team player, although he/she does a good job.

TOTAL SCORE: _____

OTHER
Now add your own reasons for why an employee
is difficult and add that to your total score:

31. _____   _____
32. _____   _____
33. _____   _____
34. _____   _____
35. _____   _____

Rating System

Think of the results of this quiz like a ship's manifest report that can
help you deal with the different types of employees you'll encounter
during your cruise through the sometimes smooth and sometimes
choppy seas of the workplace. It's a guide to the overall difficulty of
working with one or more of your employees. The lower the score,
the better your employees are to work with; the higher the score, the
more they cause problems in your company. Use the results to help
assess how bad your employee or employees really are and what you
can do about it.

   0–10 = You have a great employee or team of employees. Are
            you really sure they are that great?
  10–19 = Generally, you've got a good employee or set of em-
            ployees. There are just a few rough spots here and
            there.
  20–29 = You are starting to have difficulties with bad employees,
            but try to work through your problems before you give
            up the ship.
  30–39 = You've got serious problems with your crew or a partic-
            ularly bad employee. Time to seriously deal with your
            problems or consider firing one or more employees.
  40–59 = S.O.S.! S.O.S.! You could be in for a crash with your
            current crew.
  60 + = A sinking ship! This is definitely a disaster. Get ready
            to pull out the lifeboats and abandon ship, or take on
            an emergency crew to stay afloat.

Knowing How to Deal

As the stories in the previous chapters have illustrated, it can be difficult to figure out what to do when dealing with a particular employee, and there are several possible alternatives in any given situation. You have to take many factors into consideration, and an optimal solution isn't always possible; rather, you have to pick the most reasonable alternative at the time. To help you decide, factor in your office culture; personal style; the employee's employment history (how long on the job, any previous problems); how serious the breach; the importance of the employee's work; and how easy it will be to find a replacement, should you be considering termination. The best solution for you may be different from what it might be for someone else in a similar situation in a different workplace.

For example, you may be more willing to give an employee who has previously done good work another chance if he or she is willing to take steps to improve. But someone else may feel so angry at an employee's actions in a high-pressure work culture that he or she prefers to terminate the employee and obtain the necessary documentation to show a good reason for doing so. In other cases, loyalty to a long-term friendship with an employee or an employee's well-connected relationship with your boss or company owner may trump your inclination to fire that worker for cause. So you might have to find other alternatives, such as increased training to improve performance or restructuring the job to give critical responsibilities to someone else.

Thus, you have to think through each situation differently. Once you have a greater understanding of the situation and the range of options available, you can better decide what to do. The "What Should You Do?" questions in each chapter should get you started by giving you some possibilities to consider, especially when you find parallels with your own trials and tribulations with a particular employee. While some alternatives are obviously wrong choices, likely to not work, others could be real options. Thus, while I have provided suggestions on what to do, what someone should do or should have done will vary in any given situation depending on a number of circumstances—from workplace dynamics and office politics to an employee's work history, experience, and personality. While one approach may be ideal for some people, that approach might not work as well for someone else.

Consider my suggestions to be like well-reasoned, common sense possibilities for success in dealing with a difficult employee, although other reasonable alternatives might still exist that could lead to success. In short, there is no exact science in determining the best approach for dealing with a difficult employee—just as you can't pick exactly the best way to promote good relationships, solve problems, or resolve workplace conflicts. Group relationships and the work environment with its mix of personalities, rules, regulations, customs, politics, and changing situations are too complex for simplistic, one-size-fits-all solutions. The same holds true for how you manage your employees. There are guidelines and choices that may contribute to a better likelihood for success in handling a problem employee, but no firm "yes," "no," "do this," "do that" formulas that are certain to work.

Still, the methods presented in this book can help you better understand the dynamics of what's going on and prompt you to come up with a good choice for dealing with the problem employee. You can apply these different approaches, as appropriate, in dealing with the problem or advising a friend or associate what they can do if they have a difficult employee.

Accordingly, this last chapter is a discussion about difficult employees in general and what to do about them in different circumstances. Then, adapt this repertoire of methods to your particular situation, using different tools for strategizing and visualizing alternatives, and choosing the one you feel is right for you.

When Employees Go Bad

Employees can turn into the employee from hell for many reasons. However, the difficult employee in one workplace environment may not be difficult in another, due to different workplace cultures and expectations, as well as your personal preferences for employee behavior as a manager. So while one manager or company owner may find an employee's actions perfectly acceptable, another may find those personal qualities or actions objectionable. For example, you may like an employee who can work independently with little direction; you don't care that this person isn't a team player and doesn't get along well with other employees. What's most important to you is the employee's productivity, and you can readily find tasks the employee can do on his or her own, even putting the employee in a separate room where they can work on their own. But another boss in a different setting may find such an employee wreaks havoc in the workplace and undermines morale, because the work he or she oversees requires team work and cooperation, and this kind of loner employee is a disaster for the team.

So a bad employee for one person may be a good employee for another. It also may be possible to improve a situation by changing the conditions of the employee's work to take advantage of his or her strengths, but in other cases, you can't make such changes. Or the employee may be a disaster in most any situation, such as an employee whom you can't trust.

One way to determine what makes an employee from hell is thinking of all the things that you expect your employees to do. Again, this could vary from job to job, but a difficult employee for you is someone who doesn't do some of those things that are high on your list of expectations. For example, if your employees have to deal with the public, a bad employee is rude to customers. If technical expertise is important, the bad employee lacks the necessary skills or makes mistakes all the time.

A bad employee might have started out fine but then went over the edge—for example, when the good employee whom you allow to work independently suddenly begins to take advantage of you by repeatedly making important decisions that require your approval without checking with you first. Sometimes an employee turns difficult by taking to extremes a behavior that would otherwise be acceptable or excusable. For example, an employee may abuse the privilege to occasionally use the phone or the copier for personal reasons by repeatedly doing so. Or an employee, appreciated for his wry sense of humor, may turn into the office cut-up or start insulting others with racist or sexist humor that becomes very offensive.

While these are extremes, it helps to think of these behaviors as existing along a continuum; a good or valued employee can go bad if his or her behavior ranges too far in either direction. An occasional slip into one of these behaviors may not be enough to make someone an employee from hell, but if an employee continues to engage in those behaviors, he or she might qualify. Similarly, if an employee engages in multiple "employee from hell" behaviors, that employee may qualify even if none of these behaviors taken alone are that bad.

So what do you do? A good way to think about this question is to consider the different ways that employees can go wrong and then consider the possible responses that might be appropriate in these different situations. Accordingly, I have first listed the different ways employees can become difficult and then provided a repertoire of responses for you to choose from. And because employees may be difficult in multiple ways, you may find it useful to employ a combination of responses together or in sequence to deal with a particular situation. If one approach works to resolve the problem, fine; if not, try another. Sometimes, however, termination—of the employee's job, that is—may be the only choice.

Pick Your Problems

The following list reflects some common ways that employees go bad. One way to consider what to do about a particular employee is to think about the different behaviors and how serious they are, rating them from 0 (no problem) to 5 (major bad news), and coming up with a total. Then, you might consider how to handle the worst problems first or whether to deal with everything at the same time. Finally, you might choose from the list of strategies what to do. You'll see a matrix of problems and responses at the end of this chapter, which suggests possible responses to different problems. However, adapt what you choose based on the various factors outlined above (i.e., your work culture, your personal style, the employee's personality, the importance of the employee's work, your ability to reassign or replace the employee, etc.).

What's the Problem?	How Serious Is the Problem?					
	0	1	2	3	4	5
Too aggressive—a bully or always arguing with everyone						
Arrogant and insulting to me and others						
Insubordinate instead of following directions						
Poor at following directions; often makes mistakes						
Mentally unstable or part of a culture of violence						
A prima donna/control freak trying to take charge of others						
Incompetent—many mistakes, disorganized, difficult learning						
Claims certain skills but doesn't have them						
A know-it-all who shows off and lords it over others						
A real slow poke who takes too long to do the job						
A lazy goof-off who takes lots of time off						
Can't deal with stress and high pressure though job demands it						
Overly sensitive and emotional						

Has many personal problems interfering with work						
A busybody and gossip						
A problem with alcohol or drugs						
Calls in sick excessively						
Caught in a number of lies						
Stealing from the company						
Makes promises and doesn't keep them						
Takes credit for others' work						
Involved in criminal activity off the job						
Seems to understand but doesn't, and makes mistakes						
Always complaining and griping						
Hard to understand due to tech talk or vague explanations						
Uses office equipment and supplies for personal use						
Engages in personal or outside business activities on the job						
Can't keep a secret and shares confidential info with others						
Engages in suggestive comments/inappropriate sexual behavior						
Doesn't get along with other employees						
Other:						
Other:						

Other:						
Other:						
Other:						
TOTALS:						

Some General Guidelines for What to Do

Assessing all the reasons an employee is a problem and adding up the totals will indicate how serious the problem is; that will help you in thinking about what to do. But keep in mind that every situation is different and needs to be strategized on a case-by-case basis, considering a number of key factors:

➲ Your employee's personality and reasons for the behavior

➲ Your organization's size, culture, norms, and standards

➲ Your own personality and style of management

➲ The employee's personal relationships and alliances, if any, with others in the organization, and especially with those with power (such as your own boss and the company owner)

➲ The importance of your employee's work to the organization and whether that work can be done by others, or whether the employee is easily replaceable.

➲ How other employees feel about the employee's behavior

Before you consider specifics, though, here are some general guidelines to keep in mind when deciding how to respond. Weigh how these different factors might apply in your own situation.

Problem Personality Traits

Some problem traits might include:

➲ Too aggressive—a bully or always arguing with everyone

➲ Arrogant and insulting to you and others

➲ A prima donna/control freak trying to take charge of others

➲ A know-it-all who shows off and lords it over others

➲ A busybody and gossip

➲ Always complaining and griping

➲ Doesn't get along with other employees

➲ Engages in suggestive comments/inappropriate sexual behavior

Where there is a pattern of personality or behavior traits that make others uncomfortable, an initial strategy might be to have an individual discussion with the employee where you explain what the problem is for others in the office and for you. It may be that the problem employee isn't aware of his or her behavior's negative affect on others, so a first step is to make the person conscious of what they are doing so they can change. Once the person is aware, they have to show a willingness to change, if this approach is going to work. So you might provide some support to help motivate the person to be open to change. Depending on the situation, you can do this yourself or involve one or two other employees with whom the problem employee works well to help that employee, such as by providing feedback when the employee engages in a certain kind of negative behavior.

The difficult employee might also be referred to HR or to an outside counseling or support group for help in changing a particular behavior. Then if the employee changes, great! Problem solved. If not, look at other possible solutions that might work in your office setting, such as giving the employee work he can do on his own or relocating the employee to another office where she can work more independently. Still another approach might be to try to help your other employees feel less bothered by the behavior, if the employee is otherwise doing good work. Certainly, an employee who continues to disturb other employees with negative and disruptive behavior might ultimately have to be terminated, but consider other approaches first, as long as the employee is productive apart from the problem behavior.

Serious Personal Problems

Some serious personal problems that can disrupt the workplace occur when an employee:

➲ Is mentally unstable or part of a culture of violence

➲ Has many personal problems interfering with work

➲ Has a problem with alcohol or drugs

➲ Calls in sick excessively

➲ Is overly sensitive and emotional

Here the response depends on how serious these personal problems are and whether they pose a threat to you or the workplace. In some cases, a private talk with the employee, where you try to be sympathetic and probe for the underlying problem, might help in determining what to do. For example, if an employee has an alcohol or drug problem, maybe you can help them find an appropriate treatment program—and some companies do provide such programs. If an employee is often sick, that could be a medical problem that needs treatment, or it may be psychological, in that the employee is a hypochondriac. Still another possibility is that the employee just doesn't like the job and is finding excuses not to come to work—or the employee is being irresponsible and would rather take off and do something else.

By having a serious talk, you may be able to find out the reason and deal with that, such as by getting the employee needed help, or terminating an employee who is not right for the job or is irresponsible. If the employee is having a lot of personal problems, maybe you could suggest some possibilities for dealing with them or getting help. Possibly some time off might be what the employee needs to get his or her personal life under control. Or perhaps setting up a part-time work arrangement might be possible solution. But if the problems seem too severe and are likely to continue, then maybe termination is in order.

In short, when dealing with personal problems, assess whether you can help the employee deal with or maintain control over them while at work. If so, perhaps with your support and some support from other employees, the employee can overcome these problems. Alternatively, avoid the trap of becoming too supportive and creating a codependent relationship in the workplace. Remember, you have to put the needs of the business first, and if you can't help the employee become an effective, productive worker, generally, you have to let that employee go. If you do decide to terminate for personal issues, try to explain this decision to them as gently as possible because they already have many difficult problems in their life.

Difficulties in Doing the Job

Among the reasons that an employee may have difficulty doing the job are:

➲ Poor at following directions; often makes mistakes

➲ Incompetent—many mistakes, disorganized, difficult learning

➲ A real slow-poke who takes too long to do the job

➲ Unable to deal with stress and high pressure though job demands it

If the difficulties involve task performance, a good approach is to find out why the employee is performing poorly and provide additional support and training to help the employee do a better job. For example, if an employee is poor at following directions, it may be because he isn't listening well or because she needs the directions explained in a more detailed or concrete way. If the employee seems to be incompetent and makes many mistakes, it may be because he wasn't properly oriented to the job and may need more explanation. If the employee is disorganized, perhaps some training in how to set up systems might help. If the employee has difficulty learning, perhaps some repetition or hands-on training might work. For a slow poke, maybe she is slow because she isn't sure of what she is doing if the job has a number of steps and she just needs more practice. Or possibly teaming that employee up with another more experienced employee could help him better learn what to do.

In other words, some extra help and support might help to bring the employee up to speed. But if such help and support won't work—or doesn't after you have tried this approach—it may be there just isn't a good fit of the employee and the job, such as when an employee in a high-pressure job that requires extensive multi-tasking can't handle the stress. If you do find a poor fit that can't be remedied, again the solution is termination. But handle this diplomatically, such as by assuring the employee that he or she will do better in a job more suited to his or her aptitude.

Poor Attitude Problems

Among the attitude problems that contribute to bad behavior are:

➲ Insubordinate instead of following directions
➲ A lazy goof-off who takes lots of time off

When attitude rears its ugly head, you are dealing with a more serious problem than when an employee is simply not suited to the job. At the one extreme, you may have an employee who not only fails to follow directions properly, but also challenges your authority. At the other extreme, you may have an employee who is not motivated to work effectively and productively. Whatever the reason for the problem, you have to set limits and show who's in charge. If the employee isn't willing to adapt his or her behavior after an initial warning, it's probably best to say goodbye. On the one hand, you don't want to be locked in a power struggle with an employee who may repeatedly undermine you. On the other, you don't want an unmotivated employee draining your energy and being a drag on other employees as well.

Trust Problems

Among the trust issues that might come up are when an employee:

➲ Claims certain skills but doesn't have them.
➲ Is caught in a number of lies.
➲ Makes promises and doesn't keep them.
➲ Takes credit for others work.
➲ Can't keep a secret and shares confidential information with others.

Trust problems can be very serious, even if the particular lie or deceit is a small one, because they often point to a continuing pattern of behavior that will get worse and worse. If you catch the problem early, it might be worth giving the employee a warning, such as when an employee first makes a promise and doesn't keep it or makes a first slip by sharing confidential information (as long as he or she doesn't share extremely important information that is clearly considered secret). Even exaggerating one's skill set might merit a warning. But if you do give a warning, make it clear that you consider the violation of trust very serious and the next time there will be no warning; the employee will be asked to leave.

However, if the breach of trust is sufficiently severe, it may be best to give no warning and simply say it's over. That's because there are certain breaches that everyone understands are simply wrong—no ifs, ands, and buts—such as blatantly plagiarizing someone's work and claiming it as his or her own, or trying to get away with a big lie, such as claiming a degree one hasn't earned or concealing a serious criminal record.

"It's-a-Crime" Problems

Some common crime problems that may occur are:

➲ Stealing from the company
➲ Being involved in criminal activity off the job
➲ Using office equipment and supplies for personal use
➲ Engaging in personal or own business activities on the job

As in the case of trust problems, consider these serious breaches, although there might be some mitigating circumstances or a fudge factor involved with respect to determining when something becomes a crime. For example, if someone is stealing money or products from the company, that's clearly a crime and merits firing, and possibly criminal prosecution—if the local police or district attorney consider it serious enough and have enough evidence to proceed. However, there could be a question of when using office equipment or supplies for personal use, or engaging in personal or business activities on the job, rises to the level of being a crime. Such activities are often done as a matter of convenience, and employees are given some leeway to engage in these activities on a limited basis. But if an employee starts taking extensive supplies, that becomes a crime. And turning the workplace into one's own personal business fiefdom is clearly a violation of the conditions of employment.

An issue here can be the amount of information you have about what the employee is doing, and whether you have sufficient evidence of what you believe the employee is doing wrong. If you aren't sure and are just suspicious, you might further monitor the situation yourself or hire a private eye to do more checking for you. Then, when you are sure, confront the employee with the evidence you have and use that as a basis to fire the employee for cause.

In the case of someone involved in criminal activity off the job, consider the seriousness of the act and whether someone has been convicted or has only been accused. For example, if the criminal accusation or conviction is for something minor, like a brawl in a local bar or drunken driving causing an accident, you might start with a warning. But if the action is serious, particularly if it involves a matter of trust, such as a conviction for shoplifting or theft, by all means end the employment.

Communication Problems

You have a communication problem when the employee:

➲ Seems to understand but doesn't, and makes mistakes.

➲ Is hard to understand due to tech talk or vague explanations.

When communication problems arise, the initial strategy should be to work on making things clearer to the employee and helping the employee make what he or she is communicating clearer to you. For example, if an employee seems to understand but doesn't, and thus makes mistakes, the problem could be that the employee is afraid to say he or she doesn't understand. If that's the case, show that you want your employee to feel comfortable saying "I don't know" or "I don't understand," so you can further explain and clarify. Or if the employee *thinks* he or she understands but doesn't, try having the employee repeat back to you his or her understanding after you give instructions to make sure he or she understands—and if not, explain again. Or try hands-on demonstrations and trial practices to be sure the employee has fully internalized what to do.

While such clarification strategies can help to clear up most communication problems, in some cases a communication breakdown about skills and tasks could be an indication that the employee really isn't up to the job. If so, consider a job reassignment. Or if there is no where else to put the employee, that's a good cause for termination.

In the case of using specialized languages, this may be a problem in certain fields, where employees may know more than those in management about what they are doing. So the problem isn't that the employee doesn't know what he or she is doing, but rather that he or she has a problem conveying information about it so you understand. One approach here might be to learn more yourself about this parallel universe of tech talk in the workplace. Or perhaps you can find an employee who can act as a translator to turn tech into something you can understand. Another approach is to have the employee draw you pictures or diagrams. You may find that this is really a great employee; you just have to find a way to better figure out what the employee is saying or help that employee better convey the information to you.

Some Techniques for Making a Good Decision

Making a good decision starts with understanding what's going on, a process you can perform rationally or by using your intuition. Then, with these insights, you can draw on a repertoire of tools and techniques to help you determine what to do. Here's a look at some of the tools you might use:

Visualize possible options and outcomes. You can use visualization to imagine different scenarios for dealing with your employee and the possible outcomes. Then, choose the outcome that seems your best alternative at the time. To use visualization or mental imaging, first get very relaxed and comfortable. Find a quiet place to do this. Next, imagine you are watching film in your mind's eye and that you are the movie director. Try different responses and let the scene play out without trying to direct it yourself.

Use visualization for goal setting, preparation, and planning. Say you have already come up with an alternative, such as having a frank conversation with your employee who happens to be especially sensitive and emotional. Then, think about your desired outcome (i.e., getting the employee to accept criticism; making the employee feel confident she can take on more responsibility; suggesting ways the employee can better get along with another employee he has been in conflict with, etc.). Next, with this chosen outcome in mind, think about how to best approach your employee and what to say. One way to visualize these steps is to see a path to your goal with a series of stops or signposts along the way. Then, as you get to each stop, visualize what you will do at that location.

You can combine any of these steps with affirmations, self-talk, or other types of reinforcements to help you feel more powerful and confident when you put these actions into practice, such as when you are dealing with an employee who tends to be argumentative and manipulative. For instance, say you want to talk to your employee about how to better approach a customer and that employee becomes defensive and tries to show why he or she did it right. You might see yourself calling that employee into your office and practicing what you will say in your mind. Then, you might conclude the visualization by telling yourself, "I will be persuasive and convincing," or "The employee will be more accepting and understanding of what I have to say."

Weigh the positives and negatives to do what's practical. Another way to decide what to do and how to do it is to make a positive/negative, cost/benefit, or pro/con analysis. You can do this systematically by listing the pros and cons for each alternative you are considering to deal with your employee, using weighted ratings to compare and contrast them. Or you can make this assessment using a more intuitive, instant analysis. In this case, list each alternative, get very relaxed, and let your unconscious give you a rating from 1 (low) to 10 (high) on how practical each action would be.

Use the E-R-I Model for resolving conflicts with your employee. If you are having a conflict with your employee or are dealing with an especially defensive and emotional employee, the "E-R-I" Model (where "E-R-I" stands for the Emotions, Reasons, and Intuition) can help.

➲ *The first step is to get the negative* emotions *out of the way.* Do this by either getting your own emotions under control or listening calmly while your employee vents to express his or her anger or frustrations (such as feeling she is always being blamed for something or believing someone else who doesn't like her has made a false accusation). This way, you detach yourself from the situation so you don't get upset, yell back at your employee, or hurl angry, blaming accusations, which will only further increase the tension. Instead, you want to remain calm, focused, and in control—a little like the cop who stands by, listening to the invective of an angry motorist. But instead of getting angry, too, the cop just lets the vituperation wash over him and drain away, and generally, the motorist calms down after getting the anger out. Treat an upset employee in a similar way so you can rationally deal with the issue. However, if the problem is that the employee repeatedly erupts in this way, and you can't help him or her get that behavior under control, that could be a good reason for terminating that employee.

➲ *In step two, use your deductive* reasoning *to understand the reasons for the conflict by thinking about the different factors that contribute to it,* such as your employee's personality and responsibilities or your workplace culture and conditions. Use your reason to understand the different resolution styles you might use to resolve a conflict. In dealing with an employee, you can always use the first conflict resolution method, which is *confrontation,* where you exercise your power to seek what you want because you are the boss. But the other four conflict resolution methods might work well in different situations, particularly if you want to get the employee to express his concerns and work out a resolution that may incorporate input from this employee and others in the workplace. It may take longer to come to a resolution, but it may be a more satisfactory one that helps to support employee motivation and morale. You can use visualization to think about which approach to use to decide what to do. These are:

1. *Collaboration,* where you and other parties to the conflict take time to consider the different issues and resolve them together.

2. *Compromise,* where you each give a little.

3. *Accommodation,* where you give in to what someone else wants because they have more power or the issue isn't that important to you.

4. *Avoidance,* where you choose not to deal with the conflict by seeking to leave, not thinking about it, or delaying any action.

➲ *Finally, in step three, as you think about applying these different conflict styles, use your* intuition to brainstorm different alternatives and choose among them.

The Range of Strategies for Dealing with a Problem

The basic strategies, used individually or in combination, include the following. Consider them a basic repertoire of approaches for dealing with a difficult employee. Then, select from among them which to use and in what order, although most typically, use the least serious interventions first and scale up to the more serious ones if the first approaches don't work.

➲ Have an individual conversation with your employee.

➲ Schedule a formal employee review meeting, even if it's not time for a regular biannual or annual review.

➲ Have a discussion about the problem at a meeting with the employee and others who are involved in the situation.

➲ Bring up the problem at a staff meeting.

➲ Consult with other managers or your own boss about what to do.

➲ Put the employee on probation for a certain time period (e.g., two weeks, three weeks, one month, two months, etc.).

➲ Assign another, more experienced employee to work with and mentor that employee.

➲ Write up clearer guidelines for the employee—as well as other employees—to follow.

➲ Provide more training yourself.

➲ Provide the employee with more training through a company or outside training program.

➲ Provide the employee with some hands-on experience in the field while you or another employee observe.

➲ Ask the employee to submit periodic reports to you about how he or she is seeking to change.

➲ Give the employee a warning with a time limit (e.g., one week, two weeks, one month) of when the employee has to show significant improvement, or you will terminate his or her employment.

➲ Terminate employment as gently as you can, and provide the employee with an explanation, pay for hours already worked, and severance pay.

➲ Terminate employment immediately, explain the cause, and provide pay for any hours already worked.

➲ Report the employee's criminal actions to the appropriate authorities.

➲ Be cautious about the potential for retaliation by an angry or mentally disturbed employee, and seek a restraining order or other protections if necessary.

Putting It All Together

To sum up, a good way to approach any problem with a difficult employee is by first carefully examining the situation to determine what's going on, taking into consideration various factors including:

➲ The employee's work history and history of previous problems

➲ The employee's relationship with you and others in the workplace

➲ The seriousness of the problem

➲ The effect of the problem on other employees

Also, consider the nature of the problem, i.e., whether this is:

➲ A problem with work skills that might be corrected with training

➲ A difficulty due to personal problems or personality or behavior factors that might be corrected with some guidance and support

➲ A problem with communication that might be corrected by clearer communication

➲ An attitude, trust or criminal matter that might be dealt with by certain types of intervention or is grounds for immediate termination, and possibly further legal action or a report to law enforcement

Then, look at the various techniques you might use to help you choose and implement a particular approach. Use the Dealing with Difficult Employees Grid in the Appendix to help you in reviewing the options for different situations.

The stories in this book are examples of how others have dealt with difficult employees in different situations, and their experiences may help you figure out what to do in your own situation. In future books, I'll feature other workplace stories, from dealing with bad employees, to dealing with difficult coworkers, bosses, customers, and problem situations in general. I invite you to send in your own stories to be used in future books; I will seek to help you resolve your problem in a personal response.

The Major Techniques for Dealing with Difficult Employees

To summarize the major techniques to apply in dealing with difficult employees, here they are one last time in brief. Feel free to add your own thoughts as well. The major techniques are:

1. Assess the different factors contributing to the situation.
2. Consider possible options and outcomes.
3. Use visualization for imagining implementing different approaches and desired results.
4. Decide on the best option by weighing positives and negatives and getting a gut-level feeling of what might be best to do, given the circumstances.
5. Use the E-R-I Model for resolving conflicts or dealing with a difficult employee who's angry or upset.
6. Clear up communication problems by asking questions for clarification or providing a more detailed explanation yourself.
7. Explain your decision and what the employee needs to do to improve his/her performance or relationship, personality, or behavior problems—or explain as diplomatically as possible why you have decided to terminate the employee.

Today's Take-Aways

☑ Think about how the general principles might apply in your situation, but keep in mind that every bad employee situation is different.

☑ Use the examples of what others have done in dealing with their own bad employees to consider possible approaches for your own case, then adapt those solutions to your situation.

☑ Begin by thinking about the situation so you really understand what's going on; then, consider the various factors that may impact on the problem and what you might do to solve it.

☑ Once you understand what to do, think of the options you might use, and consider the pros and cons of different approaches.

☑ Use visualization or mental imaging to help determine possible options and outcomes; then, choose which alternative would be best for you.

Appendix:
Dealing with Difficult Employees Grid

What's the Problem (these could be reorganized into the major categories of problems, i.e., personality traits, personal problems, and skill, attitude, trust, crime, communication problems)	OPTIONS TO RESOLVE PROBLEM																	
	Conversation	Formal Review	Group Discussion	Staff Meeting	Consult Other Mgrs	Probation	Assign Mentor	Clearer Guidelines	Training by Self	Training Program	Hands-On Experience	Employee Reports	Warning & Time Limit	Termination & Severance	Immediate Termination	Report to Authorities	Retaliation Precautions	Other
Too aggressive—a bully or always arguing with everyone																		
Arrogant and insulting to me and others																		

213

	Insubordinate instead of following directions	Poor at following directions; often makes mistakes	Mentally unstable or part of a culture of violence	A prima donna/control freak trying to take charge of others	Incompetent—many mistakes, disorganized, difficult learning	Claims certain skills but doesn't have them	A know-it-all who shows off and lords it over others	A real slow poke who takes too long to do the job

- A lazy goof-off who takes lots of time off
- Can't deal with stress and high pressure though job demands it
- Overly sensitive and emotional
- Has many personal problems interfering with work
- A busybody and gossip
- A problem with alcohol or drugs
- Calls in sick excessively
- Caught in a number of lies
- Stealing from the company
- Makes promises and doesn't keep them

Takes credit for others' work	Involved in criminal activity off the job	Seems to understand, but doesn't, and makes mistakes	Always complaining and griping	Hard to understand since uses tech talk or vague explanations	Uses office equipment and supplies for personal use	Engages in personal or own business activities on the job	Can't keep a secret and shares confidential info with others	

Engages in suggestive comments/ inappropriate sexual behavior						
Doesn't get along with other employees						
Other:						
Other:						
Other:						
Other:						
Other:						

Index

abrasive employees
  arrogance in, 19–22
  toughness in, 3–7
absenteeism, 185
abusive bosses, 185
accommodation, in conflict resolution, 208
affirmations, 207
aggressive bosses, 184
aggressive employees
  guidelines for dealing with, 199–200
  as problem, 3–7
alcohol abuse
  guidelines for dealing with, 201
  as problem, 95–98
alternatives in decision making, 194–195
appearances, deceptive, 133
aptitude, employees lacking, 53–57
arrogant employees
  guidelines for dealing with, 199–200
  as problem, 19–22

attitude problem(s)
  arrogance as, 19–22
  with cultural misfits, 23–27
  guidelines for dealing with, 203
  inappropriate sharing of information as, 34–39
  negativism as, 28–33
  prima donnas with, 14–18
  rating, 189
  threatening as, 8–13
  toughness as, 3–7
avoidance, in conflict resolution, 208

background checks
  to avoid con artists, 130–131
  to avoid scams, 137–138
bad bosses, 183–187
  factors contributing to, 184–185
  signs of, 183–184, 186–187
bad employees
  employer's responsibility for, 183
  factors in creation of, 195–196

impact of, *vii*
optimum approach to dealing
   with, *viii, see also* dealing with
   bad employees
pattern or series of, 183, 184
self-assessment quiz for,
   188–192
as situationally defined, *vii–viii*
blame, accepting, 183, 184
bonding among employees, protection of incompetents and,
   67–72
boss
   complaining to, 6, 66
   employee behavior in absence
      of, 172–176
   employees protected by, 63–66
   as problem, 183–187
boundaries, unclear, 186
breaches of confidence, 34–39
bullies, 19–22

camaraderie among employees
   and prima donnas, 14–18
   and protection of incompetents,
      67–72
chain of command, unclear, 167,
   171
co-dependent relationships, 80
collaboration, in conflict resolution, 208
communication problem(s)
   of bosses, 184, 185
   in customer service, 177–180
   guidelines for dealing with,
      205–206
   inappropriate sharing of infor-
      mation as, 34–39

with inarticulate, hard-to-talk-
   to employees, 163–166
misunderstandings as, 153–157
rating, 191
technical language as, 158–162
in termination process, 167–171
when boss is away, 172–176
compassion, lack of, 184
compensation
   demands for, from position of
      power, 125–129
   inappropriate revelation of,
      36–38
   misunderstandings about,
      153–157
   precedents in, 143
competence, rating, 189–190, *see
   also* incompetence
complainers, *see* negative employees
complaining to boss, 6, 66
compromise, in conflict resolution,
   208
con artists, 130–134
concealment of major personal
   problems, 103–106
confidential information
   employees who reveal, 34–39
   guidelines for dealing with
      breaches of, 199–200, 203–204
   terminating employees who pos-
      sess, 167–170
conflict, E-R-I model for resolving,
   207–208
confrontation, 208
continuum of behaviors, 196
control, given to wrong employees,
   186
control freaks

bosses as, 184
guidelines for dealing with,
    199–200
correction, encouragement along
    with, 78
cost/benefit analysis, 207
credit
    lack of, 185
    taking, for others' work,
        203–204
crime-related problems
    criminal activity by boss as, 185
    criminally-connected employees
        as, 8–13
    guidelines for dealing with,
        204–205
critical information
    concealed from owner/manager,
        172–176
    terminating employees who pos-
        sess, 167–170
criticism, sensitivity to, 75, 78
cultural misfits, 23–27
culture, as factor in solutions, 193
customer service
    going to inappropriate extremes
        in, 177–180
    lack of skill in, 60

dealing with bad employees,
    193–212
    alternatives for, 193–194
    evaluating seriousness of prob-
        lems in, 196–199
    and factors creating difficult be-
        havior, 195–196
    general guidelines for, 199–206
    making good decisions in,
        206–208

options grid for, 210, 213–217
range of strategies for, 208–210
Dealing with Difficult Employees
    Grid, 210, 213–217
deceptive appearances, 133
decision making
    alternatives in, 194–195
    techniques for, 206–208
    by temporary managers,
        172–176
demands from position of power,
    124–129
difficult employees, *see* bad em-
    ployees
direction, lack of, 184
disadvantaged employee pro-
    grams, 8–13
dishonesty
    escalating, 118–123
    rating, 190–191
    see also trust issue(s)
disorganized bosses, 184
diversity, 23
documentation
    to avoid scams, 138
    with seriously-threatening em-
        ployees, 13
    when employee is protected by
        boss, 65
drinking problems
    employees with, 95–98
    guidelines for dealing with, 201
drug problems
    employees with, 8, 91–94, 97
    guidelines for dealing with, 201

emotional bosses, 184
emotional employees, guidelines
    for dealing with, 201

Emotions, Reasons and Intuition
    (E-R-I) Model, 207–208
empathy, lack of, 184
employers
    as problem, *see* bad bosses
    variability in behaviors accept-
        able to, 195
    see also boss
employment history, as factor in
    solutions, 193
E-R-I Model, 207–208
escalating dishonesty, 118–123
ex-convicts, 8–13
expectations for employees, 195
extortion, 128, *see also* demands
    from position of power

family members, incompetent,
    58–62
fault, admitting, 183
favors that backfire, 140–144
feedback
    for employees with personal
        problems, 83
    to friends about favors, 143
    from other employees, 71
    from references, 130
Field of Dreams motto, 118
freelance workers, 167, 168, 170
friends
    doing favors for, 140–144
    incompetent, 58–62

goals, visualizing, 206–207
government regulations, taking
    advantage through, 135–139
group interventions, *see* strength-
    in-numbers approach
group relationships, 194

guidelines for problems, 199–206
    with attitude, 203
    with communication, 205–206
    with crime, 204–205
    with difficulties in doing job,
        202
    with personality traits, 199–200
    with serious personal issues,
        200–202
    with trust, 203–204

hands-off management style, 186
hard-to-talk-to employees,
    163–166
hiring process
    laxness in, 169–170
    warning signs in, 70
honesty, *see* trust issue(s)

identifying problems and causes,
    186–187
ignoring behavior
    of arrogant employees, 21–22
    of negative employees, 32
importance of employee's work, as
    factor in solutions, 193
impulsive bosses, 185
inappropriate behavior
    in customer service, 177–180
    incentives to change, 180
    rating, 191
    sexual, 107–110
    in sharing of information, 34–39
inarticulate employees, 163–166
incentives
    to change inappropriate behav-
        ior, 180
    to change negative employees,
        32

incompetence
  and bonding and camaraderie among employees, 67–72
  of friends or family members, 58–62
  and getting passed from manager to manager, 48–52
  guidelines for dealing with, 202
  of interns, 43–47
  from lack of skill set or aptitude for job, 53–57
  and protection by boss, 63–66
  rating, 189–190
indecisive bosses, 185
inflexible bosses, 184
information-sharing employees, 34–39
ingratiating employees, prima donnas as, 14–18
instruction, lack of, 184
insufferable employees, 19–22
insulting bosses, 185
insurance settlements, 135
interns
  inarticulate, 163–164
  incompetent, 43–47
intuition, in E-R-I model, 207, 208
invasive bosses, 185

job descriptions, 56

Labor Board, 136
lateness, 185
lawsuits, 135
legal actions, employees taking, 135–139
limits, setting
  for employees with personal problems, 84

for interns, 46
little things, dishonesty in, 118–123
lying
  by boss, 185
  by employees, 113–117
  guidelines for dealing with, 203

managers, temporary, 172–176
manipulative bosses, 184
mental imaging, 206–207
mentally unstable employees
  guidelines for dealing with, 201
  as problem, 8–13
micromanagers, 184
misunderstood communications
  guidelines for dealing with, 205–206
  as problem, 153–157
monitoring
  of cultural misfits, 25
  to determine employee experience, 133–134
  and dishonesty in little things, 118
  of interns, 46
  lack of, 185
  of negative employees, 31
  of newly-promoted employees, 16–17
  and pathological liars, 116–117
  of stressful/multi-tasking positions, 89
  of threatening employees, 12–13
moonlighting, 145–149
morale, 185
multi-tasking, inability to manage
  guidelines for dealing with, 202
  as problem, 85–90

negative employees
  guidelines for dealing with,
    199–200
  as problem, 28–33
negatives, weighing positives vs.,
    207
nosy bosses, 185

obnoxious employees
  arrogance in, 19–22
  toughness in, 3–7
options, visualizing, 206
organized bosses, 184
outcomes, visualizing, 206
outside sales, miscommunications
    about, 153–157
overly-sensitive employees, 75–79

paperwork, mandatory require-
    ments for, 138
patterns of problems, 183, 184,
    186–187
payment policies
  problems with, *see* compensation
  revealing, 36–38
perfectionists, 184
personality problems, guidelines
    for dealing with, 199–200, *see
    also* attitude problem(s)
personal problem(s)
  concealment of, 103–106
  difficult life situations as, 80–84
  drinking as, 95–98
  drug use as, 91–94
  guidelines for dealing with,
    200–202
  with multi-tasking and stress,
    85–90
  over-sensitivity as, 75–79

overuse of sick time as, 99–102
  rating, 190
  sexual tensions as, 107–110
personal style, as factor in solu-
    tions, 193
physically powerful employees,
    8–13
planning, visualization in,
    206–207
positives, weighing negatives vs.,
    207
power
  demands from position of,
    124–129
  given to wrong employees, 186
prima donnas
  guidelines for dealing with,
    199–200
  as problem, 14–18
probationary period
  for employees with personal
    problems, 83
  for employees working at home,
    170
  to protect against incompetence,
    55
pro/con analysis, 207
productivity, 185
promotions, prima donna behavior
    and, 14–15
protection of incompetents
  by boss, 63–66
  by other employees, 67–72
  to spare boss, 104
provocative clothing, 109, 110
pushovers, bosses as, 186

rating
  of employee behavior, quiz for,
    188–192

of seriousness of problems, 196–199

reasoning, in E-R-I model, 207, 208

rebellious employees, 185

recognition, lack of, 185

reference checks, 71
  to avoid scams, 137–138
  for employees who freelance, 170
  fear of honest feedback in, 130
  for friends, 140
  unreachable, 133
  when doing favors for friends, 143

reflecting, 161

rehabilitation programs, employees in, 8–13

replacements
  as factor in solutions, 193
  for tough employees, 6

requirements, lack of clarity in, 185

responsibility
  given to wrong employees, 186
  not accepting, 183

reticence, 163–166

rigid bosses, 184

rude bosses, 185

scams, use of government regulations for, 135–139

second jobs, 145–149

secrets, employees who reveal, 34–39

seditious employees, 185

self-assessment quiz, 188–192

self-confidence, lack of, 165, 166

self-talk, 207

sensitive employees
  guidelines for dealing with, 201
  as problem, 75–79

series of problem employees, 183, 184, 186–187

seriousness of behavior, as factor in solutions, 193

sexual behaviors
  by boss, 185
  guidelines for dealing with, 199–200
  as problem, 107–110

shrinkage, 119, 120

shyness, 163–166

sick time, overuse of
  guidelines for dealing with, 201
  as problem, 99–102

skills, employees lacking, 53–57

social discomfort
  of cultural misfits, 23–27
  from lack of customer relations skills, 60
  from over-sensitivity, 75–79
  of shy or inarticulate employees, 163–166

standards, rigid, 185

stealing
  guidelines for dealing with, 204–205
  as problem, 118–123

strategies for dealing with problems, 208–210

strength-in-numbers approach
  with employees who are chronic problems, 51
  with tough employees, 5–6

stress, inability to manage
  guidelines for dealing with, 202
  as problem, 85–90

structured bosses, 184
success, signs of, 133
supervision, lack of, 186
support of employees, limiting, 82–83, 201
A Survival Guide for Working with Bad Bosses (Gini Graham Scott), 184, 188
suspension, of employees using drugs, 93–94

technical language
  guidelines for dealing with, 205–206
  as problem, 158–162
temporary managers, 172–176
termination
  of arrogant employees, 21
  of cultural misfits, 25, 26
  of employees having critical information, 167–170
  of employees lacking skills, 57
  of employees using drugs, 93
  of employees who extort, 129
  of employees who reveal confidential information, 38
  of employees who steal, 122
  employers' fear of, 48
  explaining, to other staff, 17–18
  factors influencing, 193
  of negative employees, 30–31
  of prima donnas, 17
  for promoting other business on your time, 147–148
  of seriously-threatening employees, 10–12
  unclear responsibility for, 167–171

when employee has been protected by others, 69–70
"them vs. me" situations, 26
threatening, employees who are
  in rehabilitation situations, 8–13
  through arrogance, 19–22
tough attitudes
  bosses with, 184
  employees with, 3–7
training programs
  for disadvantaged employees, 12–13
  lack of, 185
trial period, 55
troubled youths, 8–13
trust issue(s)
  with arrogant employees, 20
  with boss, 185
  and con jobs, 130–134
  demands from position of power as, 124–129
  dishonesty in little things as, 118–123
  guidelines for dealing with, 203–204
  inappropriate sharing of information as, 34–39
  lying as, 113–117
  moonlighting as, 145–149
  rating, 190–191
  use of regulations to take advantage as, 135–139
  when doing favors, 140–144
turnover, 184, 185

unclear chain of command, 167, 171
unemployment insurance, 69
unfair bosses, 185

"us vs. them" situations, 17–18

verifying employee skills, 55, 56
violent culture, employees from
    guidelines for dealing with, 201

as problem, 8–13
visualization, 206–207

weighing positives and negatives,
    207

About the Author

Gini Graham Scott, Ph.D., J.D., is a nationally known writer, consultant, speaker, and seminar/workshop leader, specializing in business and work relationships, and professional and personal development. She is founder and director of Changemakers and Creative Communications & Research, and has published more than forty books on diverse subjects. Her previous books on business relationships and professional development include: *A Survival Guide for Working with Bad Bosses, A Survival Guide for Working with Humans, Resolving Conflict* and *Work with Me! Resolving Everyday Conflict in Your Organization.* Her books on professional and personal development include *The Empowered Mind: How to Harness the Creative Force Within You* and *Mind Power: Picture Your Way to Success.*

Gini Scott has received national media exposure for her books, including appearances on *Good Morning America!, Oprah, Geraldo at Large, Montel Williams,* CNN, and *The O'Reilly Factor.* She additionally has written a dozen screenplays, several signed to agents or optioned by producers, and has been a game designer, with more than two dozen games on the market with major game companies, including Hasbro, Pressman, and Mag-Nif. Two new games are being introduced by Briarpatch in 2007.

She has taught classes at several colleges, including California State University, East Bay, Notre Dame de Namur University, and the Investigative Career Program in San Francisco. She received a

Ph.D. in Sociology from the University of California in Berkeley, a J.D. from the University of San Francisco Law School, and M.A.s in Anthropology and in Mass Communications and Organizational, Consumer, and Audience Behavior from Cal State University, East Bay.

She is also the founder and director of PublishersAndAgents.net, which connects writers with publishers, literary agents, film producers, and film agents. The four-year old service has served more than 750 clients, and has been written up in the *Wall Street Journal* and other publications.

For more information, you can visit her websites at www.ginigrahamscott.com, which includes a video of media clips and speaking engagements, and www.giniscott.com, which features her books. Or call or write to Gini Scott at her company:

Changemakers
6114 La Salle, #358
Oakland, CA 94611
(510) 339-1625
changemakers@pacbell.net